WHAT YOU WERE NEVER TOLD
The Journey from Adolescence to Adulthood

VIPUL RASTOGI

Published by
Rupa Publications India Pvt. Ltd 2024
7/16, Ansari Road, Daryaganj
New Delhi 110002

Sales centres:
Bengaluru Chennai
Hyderabad Jaipur Kathmandu
Kolkata Mumbai Prayagraj

Copyright © Vipul Rastogi 2024

The views and opinions expressed in this book are the
author's own and the facts are as reported by him which
have been verified to the extent possible, and the publishers
are not in any way liable for the same.

All rights reserved.
No part of this publication may be reproduced, transmitted,
or stored in a retrieval system, in any form or by any means,
electronic, mechanical, photocopying, recording or otherwise,
without the prior permission of the publisher.

P-ISBN: 978-93-6156-364-5
E-ISBN: 978-93-6156-022-4

First impression 2024

10 9 8 7 6 5 4 3 2 1

The moral right of the author has been asserted.

Printed in India

This book is sold subject to the condition that it shall not,
by way of trade or otherwise, be lent, resold, hired out, or otherwise
circulated, without the publisher's prior consent, in any form of
binding or cover other than that in which it is published.

For my son, Parth; for my wife; and our parents.

CONTENTS

Introduction   ix

Part 1: Life
1. The 'S' Word   3
2. Making Sense of Failures   13
3. Relationships and Dealing with Break-Ups   20
4. Social Media, Self-Esteem and Self-Confidence   30

Part 2: Health
5. What Is All the Fuss about Sleep?   45
6. Nutrition for Adolescents   52
7. Physical Fitness, Exercise and Supplements   70
8. Sex, Sexuality and Sexual Orientation   84
9. Women's Health and Contraception   96

Part 3: Careers and Finance
10. The Dreaded Exams   105
11. Career Choices and How to Make Them   114
12. The Question of Money   125

Part 4: Addictions
13. Internet and Screen Addiction   139
14. Alcohol Use   152

15. Nicotine Abuse	160
16. Drug Abuse	168
17. Coffee: The World's Favourite Drink	176

Part 5: Mind Matters

18. Mental Health: Let's Not Talk about It	183
19. Self-Harm and Suicide	195
Afterword	208
Bibliography	210
Acknowledgements	217

INTRODUCTION

What happens when the clock strikes midnight on your eighteenth birthday? Do you feel any different? Does your body feel different? Does your thinking or personality change?

More than physiological changes, the notion of adulthood is about societal perception. You can live independently, drive, open a bank account, buy property, vote, get married or have children, among other privileges.

Transitioning from adolescence to adulthood is a challenging and confusing time. There have been so many times in my own life where I have thought to myself, 'I wish I was prepared for this situation,' or 'I wish somebody had told me about this.' I wish I had had the confidence in my late adolescence to ask difficult questions, and when I had mustered up the courage to, I wish I would not have been laughed at or told that I would 'figure it out' when I grew up.

India has a very young population—about 22 per cent of the Indian population is constituted by adolescents who will, over the next 2-3 years, become adults. The World Health Organization (WHO) recognizes adolescence as 'a period of life with specific health and developmental needs and rights. It is also a time to develop knowledge and skills, learn to manage emotions and relationships, and acquire attributes and abilities that will be important for enjoying the adolescent years and assuming adult roles.'

This definition makes it evident that one's adolescent years should be focussed on learning about what is to come in life and how one can make informed choices. Unfortunately, the only thing we are expected to learn during adolescence is school curricula, and we are, more often than not, left to fill in the blanks as we go.

To be able to develop knowledge and skills, the two major sources of information available to adolescents are friends—who are usually also in the same phase of life—and the Internet. But even while using the Internet, it is essential that you access authentic and well-vetted websites or data sources to acquire information that can help you make informed decisions. As soon as you turn 18, society behaves as if a switch has been flipped and you suddenly possess the capacity to make your own decisions, whether good or bad. But is a person as young as 18 years of age, who has not had a solid grounding in making life choices, ready and prepared to assume the responsibilities of adulthood and make important, life-changing decisions?

The next part of the WHO definition of adolescence highlights the capacity 'to manage emotions and relationships'. Adolescents are rarely taught about emotions or relationships either in school or at home. The standard response to anything remotely related to relationships (especially those of a romantic nature) is the inevitable, 'This is not the time for relationships, you should focus on your studies and career.' Regrettably, when relationships fall apart in early adulthood, one is often unprepared to manage emotions because their view of relationships is distorted by what they have seen in popular media. This can lead to the development of unhealthy coping mechanisms like self-harm and substance abuse, as well as an inability to process one's emotions in a healthy manner.

In India, primary care practitioners are the main providers of healthcare information to the entire family. Some people do not have access to them, and sometimes healthcare providers are too inundated with work to dispense advice about general life matters. Medical healthcare in India is more reactive than proactive. Often, the healthcare provider does not have time or hasn't updated themself on the issues faced by adolescents. Other times, the questions raised by the adolescent may be hushed by society or made to seem either frivolous or insignificant.

The availability of psychologists in schools is helping to improve the situation, but the fear of being judged by one's teachers and peers deters a student from seeking help. They then turn to the Internet to find answers, which is not always the best option.

Everyone trains for and talks about success, but how do we manage failure? We build relationships, and relationships break. They are considered important learning curves in life, but nobody talks about how to manage them. It is a process that needs much more than 'pull up your socks' or 'it is not the time for this'.

While this book aims to answer questions that a young person might hesitate to ask, it is not an alternative to meeting professionals on a one-on-one basis if things are not going well. In difficult times, the solutions available might not be black and white. They could exist in 'the grey zone'. Talking with a professional can help you work out the best possible way to navigate difficult situations. Until then, I hope this book is able to impart some guidance.

Part 1
LIFE

'Every moment is a fresh beginning.'

—T.S. ELIOT

1
THE 'S' WORD

'Stress acts as an accelerator: it will push you either forward or backward, but you choose which direction.'

—CHELSEA ERIEAU

Stress is a well-known phenomenon, and I think no one can honestly say that they have no stress. There are many definitions for the word 'stress', but it can generally be defined as anything that stops you from giving your 100 per cent.

Stress is universal, and everyone experiences it from time to time. But not everyone is affected by stress in the same way. Some people are able to manage their stressors better than others.

But are all stressors bad? Stress is highly personal and subjective, which means that the same stress may impact different people differently. Stress could be due to personal, professional, familial, financial or legal reasons, amongst others. These are all bad stresses. However, there is good stress as well from good stressors. These are called *eustressors* and are present when one has upcoming positive life events, such as beginning a new course, starting a new job or getting married. In fact, some stressors increase our efficiency. Take, for example, the stress we feel before exams. For most students, exam stress releases adrenaline and helps then focus. However, the exact same exam stress can prove detrimental for other students.

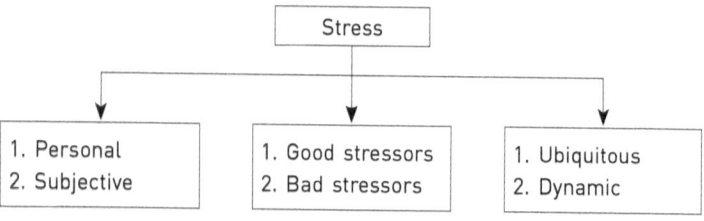

Figure 1: Different aspects of stress

It is essential to acknowledge that there is nobody with no stress. Stressors are ubiquitous as well as dynamic; some are ever present, while others change over time. Think hard about the stressors or challenges you faced five years ago; they are probably very different from what you currently face. I believe that these would change in the next five years.

Let's do an exercise. Think of some of the stressors you have in your life right now and list them below.

Stressors
1
2
3
4
5

Now, go back five years and think of the stressors you had then. Most of you would smile when you realize that the problems that had loomed large then, would be dwarfed by the pressing problems of the current day. So, we cannot really avoid stressors, but we can learn to manage them better.

Vikram is a Class 11 student who is excellent in studies, and aspires to crack the NEET exam in two years. He also wants to do well in gymnastics and has a band with his friends. His coach sees potential in him and wants him to practise for two hours every day; his bandmates also want him to practise with them for at least an hour every day. Lately, he has been more irritable than usual and has started avoiding phone calls from friends and has also started skipping school. What do you think he should do?

In my clinical practice, I have seen that most people chase perfectionism, and the pressure to do everything perfectly becomes too much to handle. The first thing to realize is that nobody is perfect at anything (let alone everything). There is always scope for improvement. Secondly, we can be good at some things but not at everything. This pressure to be great at everything and live up to unreasonably high expectations causes stress and could eventually lead to low self-esteem and self-confidence. Third, we must realize that perfection is subjective and abstract, and, perhaps more importantly, that we can be perfect only in perfect circumstances, and the world is far from perfect.

Let's talk about some practical things. Visualize a weighing scale.

On one side of the scale, put everything that you see as a stressor in your life. We need to put something that can compensate for it on the other side of the scale to create a balance. The opposite of stress is relaxation. For example, if you put something that weighs about 4 kg on the stress side, you have to balance it out with 4 kg of something relaxing on the other side. If the stress side weighs 6 kg today, you have to balance it with equal weight on the other side.

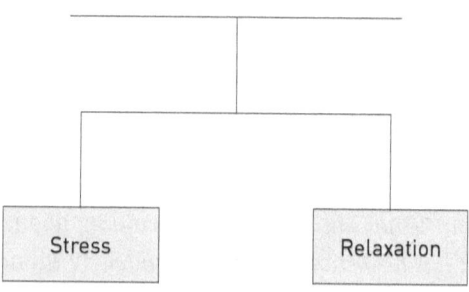

Figure 2: Balanced stress

Unfortunately, instead of increasing relaxation proportionally in real life, we begin actively reducing it, citing reasons like, 'I don't have time', or 'This is not my priority right now.' This causes a double whammy, and the weighing balance starts getting skewed. If this position is maintained for a few days, we can overcome it over days or weeks, like in the case of exams or bereavements. But if this state is prolonged, it increases our irritability, anxiety and causes stress-related headaches, which leads to sleeping poorly and feeling depressed.

Furthermore, people tend to bottle up their emotions. We all have a finite capacity to handle stress and deal with difficult emotions or challenges. Slowly but surely, this capacity gets exhausted, resulting in an outburst of anger, grief, anxiety or sadness. It is essential to avoid reaching that tipping point.

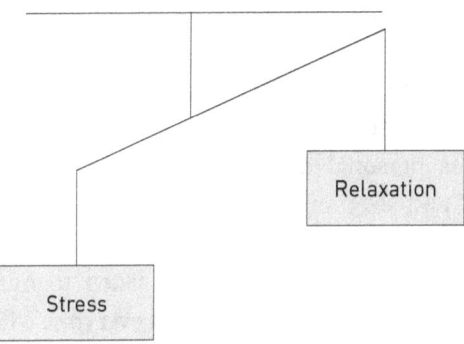

Figure 3: Imbalanced stress

Balancing the scales can help us feel better. We only have two options: either reduce the stressors or increase the time or methods for relaxation. The stressors might not be in our control or we might not be aware of their effect on us. In instances like these, we have to ensure that we have enough time dedicated to rest and relaxation to be able to correct the balance and feel better.

Let's do another exercise. Think of some strategies that you use to manage your stressors.

Strategies to Manage Stress	
1	
2	
3	
4	
5	

Coping Mechanisms

All the things that we do to make ourselves feel better and manage our difficulties are called coping mechanisms.

Stress is personal and subjective. The same applies to relaxation, and everyone has different coping mechanisms. Some people may prefer to go to the gym, while others might like to meditate. While some might listen to music, others might learn to play an instrument. Not everyone will find relief with the same coping strategy. When we talk about relaxation techniques, it is important to remember that one size does not fit all.

While the examples given above are instances of good coping habits, there are a number of unhealthy coping strategies. Some people, unfortunately, resort to anger, self-harm, alcohol, smoking or drugs to cope. You might hear them say that it helps them to relax at the end of a stressful day. This, however, is not true—the effect these substances induce is actually akin to numbness. While they may help you forget your problems for some time, they pile up on the stressors side in the long term. In many instances, they worsen strained interpersonal relationships, increase financial burdens, cause health problems, and so on. These coping strategies are called bad or maladaptive coping strategies. We will discuss in greater detail, the effect of alcohol and other substances. Similarly, avoidance behaviours, rash driving and comfort eating are all maladaptive coping behaviours. They may provide brief distractions but leave you with guilt and regret as soon as the comfort wears off, leaving you to feel worse than before.

Dev is a student of Class 12, studying in the science stream. He has grown up in a family of engineers. He is a bright student who excels in academics and generally ranks amongst the top scorers in his class. However, his scores started showing marked decline. With the board examinations drawing close, his teachers were worried. He was also disinterested in class discussions and seemed generally gloomy. His class teacher asked him to share his worries, assuring him that the conversation would remain confidential. He told her that his family members had high hopes for him and were expecting him to crack JEE (Joint Entrance Examination) in the first attempt. These expectations got too high for him. He felt isolated, being made to feel that nobody wanted to know how he felt or what he wanted.

Dev is clearly stressed, but what coping mechanisms is he using to manage that stress? It is evident that he is resorting to avoidance and is bottling up his emotions. What do you think Dev should do? Let us read further to understand.

He also shared that with the increasing pressure of board exams, JEE and his family's expectations, he had failed to strike a balance and, so, had lost enthusiasm and could not focus. When his teacher asked him about his daily routine, she was amazed to hear that he had no time for himself. What stunned her even more was that he actually felt guilty when he tried to do something relaxing. His teacher was able to counsel him and helped make a study schedule which also allowed him some time for rest and recreation. With the support of his teachers and peers, he started feeling better and his confidence rose once again. He did well in his board exams and was also able to crack JEE in his first attempt.

The strategies that help us in the long run are called good coping mechanisms. We all need to find something that works for us. We can divide good coping skills into distraction techniques and relaxation techniques. Distraction techniques help in the immediate and short term, while relaxation activities increase our resilience and tolerance to stressors in the long run.

Distraction techniques are used when we are facing a challenging situation and are struggling to cope, or when we feel anxious or might do something impulsive that we would later regret. These activities, like listening to music, taking deep breaths, counting numbers or reading a book, take your mind away from the immediate difficulty.

Managing Stress in the Long-Term

Relaxation or resilience-building activities include physical activities like sports, yoga, running or exercising at the gym, learning a musical instrument, learning a new craft, pursuing hobbies, and so on. The brain releases endorphins when we exercise or play a sport, making us feel positive and improving our confidence. However, sometimes, we get a sudden burst of motivation and push ourselves to achieve big targets in unreasonably small time gaps, resulting in fatigue and, in extreme cases, injuries. Therefore, it becomes difficult to sustain the motivation. Other times, we wait for the perfect day to begin exercising and, more often than not, that time never comes. We are then filled with more guilt and never actually get started despite making great plans.

I suggest that you begin by setting small targets. If you have five minutes, then do just five minutes of a workout or a hobby of your choice. Once you start with five minutes regularly, you can build upon it and steadily do more, but it is essential to start somewhere. The safest strategy is to go low and slow—start with low-intensity activities and build slowly.

Prioritization is essential. Depending on what is happening in our lives, we have to adapt to the changing circumstances. All of us wish that we had longer days to do what we want to, but sometimes we cannot, and that is something we must accept and learn to prioritize better.

We should take time to reflect on how the day has gone and what we could have done differently. Try to fix a routine, eat healthy and sleep well. It helps to have a tentative plan in mind for the following day. But over-reflection can make things worse. While it is difficult to strike a balance, it can be achieved with regular practice.

Vikram [the Class 11 student] eventually decided to go to band practice twice a week and, after discussing his educational commitments with his coach, agreed to an hour of daily training.

In conclusion, stress is universal and must be dealt with through good coping strategies. There will be different things that work for different people. You might have to try several methods before you find one that works for you.

Here is another exercise. What coping skills would you advise yourself to adopt?

Coping Skills	
1	
2	
3	
4	
5	

KEY POINTS

1. Be kind to yourself. Don't try to be perfect all the time.
2. Learn to say 'no'. You can't do everything.
3. Never compare. You may not be aware of what is happening in another person's life.
4. Be mindful of stressors. Anticipate them and try and plan for them.
5. There are good coping skills and bad coping skills. Invest time and energy in good coping skills.
6. Alcohol, smoking, anger and avoidance are maladaptive coping skills and must be avoided.
7. Use distractions or mindfulness techniques to let go of things in the heat of the moment.
8. Add good coping techniques like exercise and hobbies to help develop better resilience and tolerance against life stressors.

2

MAKING SENSE OF FAILURES

'Success is not final; failure is not fatal.
It is the courage to continue that counts.'

—SIR WINSTON CHURCHILL

A lack of success or not having your wishes fulfilled is usually considered a failure. But what is the definition of success, and who defines what success is? There are three essential aspects of our lives—personal life, professional/ academic life and social life. Life or success should be seen as a sum of the various aspects of life—the parts being personal, professional and social—rather than looking at them individually. Does a setback in one part of life define your life as a total failure?

Consider how you manage your own setbacks. These setbacks are not limited to examinations—they can be in relationships or on sports fields, too. Think about how differently we process our emotions when our team loses a match or we fail an examination.

A successful career cannot make up for failed relationships or not having friends. Success, just like life, should be seen in totality, but more often than not, it remains under the subjective interpretation of not just the person themselves but also of the society.

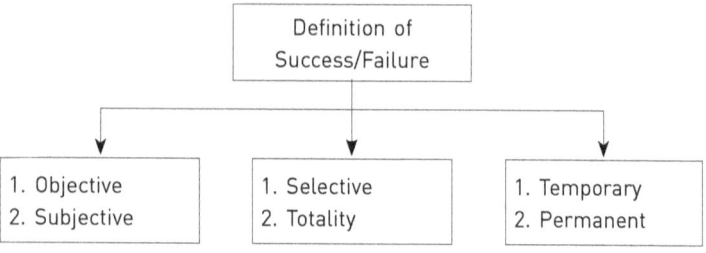

Figure 4: Different aspects of success

As a society, we appreciate success and look down on failure. Failures are the building blocks of success, and there can be no success without failure. While aspiring to become the next Bill Gates, Steve Jobs or Michael Jordan, we must remember the many failures they faced before finding their winning formula. Should you hold firm with society's estimation of your successes and failures or should you determine what success and failure look like to you?

Colonel Sanders of KFC failed in several of his endeavours before tasting success in his mid-sixties. Walt Disney went broke and had to sell his camera to pay off his debts before making it big in films. It would have seemed easier to give up, but they persisted and eventually achieved success later in their lives.

When talking about the perseverance it took to invent the lightbulb, Thomas Edison famously said, 'I have not failed. I've just found 10,000 ways that won't work.' While keeping a positive attitude in life is a must, it is important to remember that life is not sustainable without negative thoughts. A negative thought that comes into a student's mind—whether they will pass an exam or not—generally works as a motivator to work harder. If the student is overconfident, they could become complacent and not study. Therefore, a healthy mix of positive (optimistic) and negative (pessimistic) thoughts is essential for a balanced view of life.

Failing an exam or falling out of a relationship can evoke feelings of sadness, embarrassment, anger, anxiety and depression. While there persists the considerable burden of what other people will think, one also has to deal with feelings of self-resentment and the guilt of letting people down. It is not just about managing your own expectations and aspirations but also of those around you. Families tend to overestimate an adolescent's capabilities, and they themselves underestimate their abilities.

Success and failure are both subjective—a student who typically ranks in the top two positions in the class would see the third rank as a failure, and a student who didn't think they would pass would see a score of 40 per cent as success. The only measure of success should be whether you gave it your all or not. Failure shouldn't be seen as the end of the road, but as a way of knowing where you need to focus your efforts to achieve success in your endeavours.

Failures increase uncertainties in life, and these uncertainties make us feel uncomfortable. Think about how failure impacts your emotions. Does it

1. reduce your self-belief and self-worth?
2. leave you feeling like a failure in others' eyes?
3. increase your jealousy when your peers score better than you?

4. make you feel that you will never be successful in your life and, consequently, increase your insecurities?

Perhaps it is a mixture of all of the above. The bottom line is that we are all affected differently. It is, therefore, essential to channel your energy and emotions in the right direction and not give up.

A perfectionist mindset is also unfeasible; we need to acknowledge that we cannot be perfect in every circumstance and compare our outcomes with those of others. We can only be perfect in perfect situations, but can conditions ever be the same for everyone? No. Therefore, reprimanding oneself with the yardstick of another person's outcomes is pointless.

Divya, a student of Class 10, scored brilliantly in other subjects, but she failed to secure good marks in English. However, for other students, her score in English (85 per cent) was remarkable. Divya was disheartened by her score in English because it was her lowest. In all other subjects, she had done extremely well, scoring 98 per cent in a few subjects. She became disinterested in her English lessons and, instead of being more attentive, wrote herself off as 'weak' in the subject.

Her teacher picked up on this and helped her realize that she was not weak but only needed extra practice to bring her score in English at par with her performance in the other subjects. She started showing improvement once she accepted what was required and did away with her 'perfectionist mindset'.

Be a 'SMART' Student

I would typically advise students to use the '**SMART**' principle while studying. 'SMART' is an acronym for '**S**pecific', **M**easurable', '**A**ttainable', '**R**elevant' and '**T**ime-Bound'. This is a mantra used in project management. It would help if we thought of every exam as an independent project that needs to be managed. 'Specific' refers to choosing a specific area to study. Focus your energy in areas that are deemed important by your teachers. 'Measurable' means that you should be able to measure the progress you make. In the context of exams, it may mean getting better marks. 'Achievable' refers to setting realistic targets. This includes realizing that learning an entire book by rote is counterproductive and that, by trying to do this, you are setting yourself up for failure. 'Relevant' refers to doing that which is needed to complete the task at hand. For example, are you studying for the next exam or researching unnecessary material? Use your time and energy wisely. 'Time-Bound' means setting deadlines for the completion of tasks in order to prevent procrastination.

Manas promises his parents that he will be one of the top three scorers in the class in the upcoming exams. To achieve this he plans to read all the course books from cover to cover.

What do you make of his plan?

While it is very specific, measurable, relevant and time-bound, the target is arguably not achievable. Very few can memorize a book from cover to cover, let alone several books. Secondly, Manas hasn't taken into consideration the efforts of the students who are already in the top three. He seems to be setting himself up for failure here because, even if he comes in fourth, he would not have achieved what he had promised. The SMART-er thing to do here would have been to say, 'I will do better in the next set of exams than how I fared last time.' This could be as simple as saying, 'I want to score 25 per cent more than what I did in the last exam.'

Changing How We View Failure

Failure is a part of life and helps us in one way or another. But it is difficult to accept negative emotions and cope with our failure when it has just happened. Both success and failure are temporary, and the journey towards self-improvement is an eternal one.

Failures can be daunting, but they can make us more emotionally resilient and prepare us better for life. Learning how to deal with failure when we face small setbacks early in life—such as not doing well in exams or not winning in a competition that you worked hard for—prepares us to cope with bigger setbacks that we will inevitably face later in life in a healthy way.

When you read about successful people, do not forget to read about their failures, too. As the popular saying goes, 'Never tried, never failed, never achieved.' Failure means that we tried to succeed, instead of simply sitting and wondering *if* we could succeed. And, in the end, a whole-hearted attempt at success is all that matters.

KEY POINTS

1. **Accept your emotions:** It is okay to feel sad when you have a setback. It is essential to express your feelings and not bottle them up. Find motivation in your failure and use it to overcome

other challenges in life. Write about your emotions and feelings in a journal or talk to people around you about how you feel.
2. **Be mindful of irrational beliefs about failures:** One failure does not negate all the positive things or successes that you have achieved in life. While you may be given to despairing, remember that the high of success dies down after some time, and so will the disappointment of a failure.
3. **Be realistic about failure:** The only sign of success should be whether you gave it your best or not. When circumstances are not ideal, we can't expect to give our best. However, this does not mean that we can shirk our responsibilities, because there is always something we can do to improve ourselves.
4. **Develop healthy coping skills**: Use good coping skills, such as mindfulness, exercise or positive affirmations, to manage situations.
5. **Avoid bad coping skills:** Resorting to anger, self-blame or blaming others for failure is futile. If we do not take responsibility for ourselves, we cannot hope to improve.
6. **Ask yourself what you have learned from this:** Think about where you could have done better and try to do things differently next time. Put in more effort, and remember that success requires some sacrifice. Use the disappointment you feel in the moment to do better the next time.
7. **Start again soon:** Do not ponder too long over failures. Devise a plan for your next attempt and start quickly. Procrastinating and over-analysing the same thing over and over are counterproductive when it comes to achieving success. Take some time to process your feelings and start again.
8. **Never give up:** Imagine what would have happened if your parents had not let you walk or cycle because you kept falling. Success is built on patience and persistence. If you keep getting stumped on a googly, it should motivate you to practise rather than giving up playing cricket entirely.

3

RELATIONSHIPS AND DEALING WITH BREAK-UPS

*'The quality of our relationships
determines the quality of our life.'*

—ESTHER PEREL, PSYCHOTHERAPIST

Imagine how it would feel to spend a year on a beautiful island. The catch is, you're there all alone. I suspect that the initial euphoria will slowly turn into boredom and irritability over a few days, and that holiday will also start feeling like confinement.

Relationships are the building blocks of life. Every relationship that we have, including our relationships with our family members, friends, work colleagues and romantic partners, are important and serve different purposes in our lives. They are essential to us for a variety of reasons—some provide comfort, some provide security, some give us a way to manage our stressors, while others impart life lessons, help us face challenges and, of course, make us a part of the lives of others and stop us from feeling lonely. Our relationships, in the long term, help us lead a meaningful life.

Healthy Relationships: Their Importance and Impact

Relationships can be rewarding and challenging at the same time. While they are significant sources of fulfilment and happiness, they can also be sources of distress and unhappiness. A healthy and positive relationship can make us feel secure and help us grow in life, whereas a negative or toxic relationship can make us feel irritated, demotivated and helpless. It is important to remember that there is no perfect relationship, and all of them have their ups and downs.

If there is no disagreement, it could indicate that a partner is dominant. Think of a company where the boss is exceptionally dominant and puts all their employees down and does not allow them to express their ideas and opinions. What do you think the employees in that company feel? How would you feel if you were placed in a similar situation at work or in your personal life?

We are born into some relationships, such as our family; some relationships are imposed on us, as with work colleagues; and other relationships, such as friends, romantic relationships, life partners, and so on, we choose for ourselves. The choices we make, in terms of chosen relationships, often depend on common interests and dislikes. The strength of a relationship is tested when you are faced with a conflict and how you manage it. Does one run away from the relationship? Or do you try to fix it, because you think the relationship is worth it, and because of all the common interests you share?

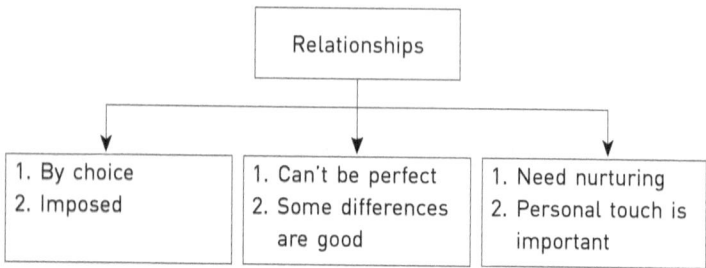

Figure 5: Different aspects of interpersonal relationships

We often measure our popularity based on the number of people we know or are 'friendly' with, a tendency that has become more pronounced because of the omnipresent virtual world and the endless possibilities it symbolizes. But empty associations, real-time or virtual, do not add actual value to our lives; healthy relationships do. Being more connected with a partner, family and friends can help you deal with challenges better and keep you in good spirits.

Relationships need to be nurtured like seeds and necessitate investment in terms of time, patience and commitment. A healthy and positive relationship is one where two people encourage, support, help and love each other.

Features of a healthy and robust relationship:

1. Trusting each other
2. Communicating openly and without the fear of being judged
3. The ability to communicate in confidence; the maintenance of privacy
4. Listening to each other with interest and undivided attention

5. Taking time out for each other exclusively and engaging in common interests and activities together
6. Encouraging each other to improve and helping each other reach ones maximum potential
7. Expressing appreciation for all things, small and large
8. Being ready to apologize and forgive—being assertive but also understanding that disappointments can come in a relationship and that they should not negate all the good things that you have achieved together

A healthy relationship brings with it a sense of well-being, a positive attitude towards life, better health, improved resilience and a tolerance to stress. An unhealthy relationship can make one feel sad, underconfident and anxious with low self-esteem.

Dealing with Loss

Relationship losses, such as bereavement in the family, the loss of a friend due to a disagreement or the breaking up of a romantic relationship, can make us feel sadness, devastation, hurt and pain. It is not just the immediate impact of the loss of the person's companionship, but also the loss of the hopes and plans that you may have had for the future. It can make one feel overwhelmed in the short term and, if unmanaged, depressed in the long run.

Avantika is a student of Class 11 (Humanities). She excels in drama, debates and dancing. In school competitions she is the life and soul of her team and generally leads her team to victory. She is well-liked by her teachers and is adored by most of her classmates, which helped her make a good circle of friends. Kriti, who is also in Class 11, has been her closest friend for the last 4–5 years. Kriti is a very bright student, excels in academics and has opted for the Science stream. With time, a large chunk of Kriti's day was being taken up by her studies and coaching, and she had started spending more time with her new batch mates. She withdrew from Avantika, who had become emotionally dependent on her over the last few years. Avantika found it challenging to manage her emotions at the tremendous loss of friendship. Not only did her scores decline, but she also withdrew herself from participating in school events. She eventually consulted the school psychologist.

The psychologist helped her deal with the emotional impact that the loss of a friendship can have on an individual. They worked through her feelings of grief, rejection and not being 'good enough', and made her see that the blame wasn't entirely hers when she held herself responsible for the change in their dynamic. The psychologist was also able to help her build an internal sense of self-validation rather than relying on other people's appreciation. This brought about a sense of acceptance in Avantika as she worked through the changes in her life.

Relationships are like roller coasters, and things don't always work out. Some relationship break-ups are contextual, that is, they break down over a specific issue. But others break down because of long-term distrust and unhappiness. Relationships that would have started with common interests, love and support from a partner may become tedious, disinteresting and frustrating due to the pressures of life, inattention and mistrust, and therefore may become dissatisfying and a source of stress. Sometimes, the initial choice of partner may not have been appropriate. For example, it may have been due to the societal pressures of marrying. Such relationships, more often than not, do not work out.

The days following a break-up are filled with a sense of guilt, regret and insecurity. The thoughts one has can vary between what one could have done differently and how it went so wrong after a promising start.

The Stages of Grief

People can go through various emotions after a relationship breakdown, and the modified Kubler-Ross model of grief can explain them.[1]

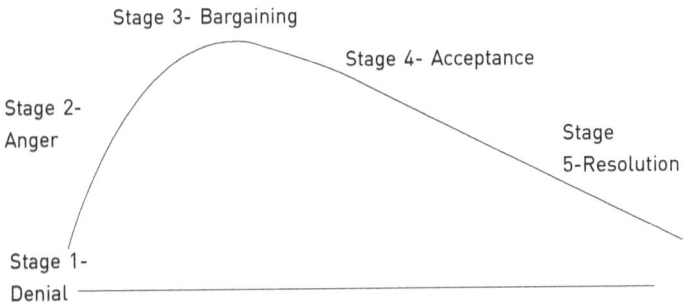

Figure 6: Modified Kubler-Ross Model of Grief

The first stage is '**denial**', where a person struggles to accept that the relationship has broken down and is surprised by the event. The second stage is '**anger**', which could be either towards the partner or the self; the former comes from a

---

[1]Tyrell, Patrick, et al., 'Kubler-Ross Stages of Dying and Subsequent Models of Grief', *StatPearls [Internet]*, 26 February 2023, http://tinyurl.com/9tshssam. Accessed on 27 December 2023.

feeling of blame and the latter stems from remorse. This anger, at its extreme, could take the form of lashing out verbally or physically, drinking alcohol or self-harm. The third stage is '**bargaining**', where the person attempts to reason away and make peace with the change that caused grief. In the case of a failed relationship, this can include accepting ones mistakes and making compromises in an attempt to get back together. The fourth stage is '**acceptance**', where one accepts that the relationship is over. There is often a feeling of helplessness at this stage. The final stage is '**resolution**', where people get on with their lives.

Every relationship is different, and people can take their own time processing break-ups and going through these stages. Not everyone will follow this graph, and, needless to say, everyone gets over break-ups on their own time and in their own way. Hurt and grief are very individual, very private experiences, and each person copes with them in their own specific ways.

However, it doesn't need to be quite so challenging to manage. While break-ups hurt a lot, proper understanding and support can help people come out of relationships unscathed and perhaps even more robust. Sometimes, leaving toxic relationships may seem impossible. We have heard of people developing Stockholm Syndrome and falling in love with the abusive partners. But people who are able to make it out feel liberated, and, after a while, have their self-esteem and confidence return.

How to look after yourself after a break-up?

1. **Accept that the relationship is over**: Mulling over it does not change the outcome. The relationship fell apart for a

reason, and if it did so because of incompatibility issues, then it is better to separate sooner rather than later.
2. **Express your feelings**: Do not bottle up your feelings. It is best to express them either by writing them or speaking to someone about them. The more you keep them inside, the more difficult it is to recover.
3. **Maintain a routine**: Try and follow your usual routine. Sitting idle and avoiding people generally makes the situation much worse. Try to be in the company of friends and be socially active.
4. **Prioritize yourself:** Make sure you eat and sleep well and do some meaningful activities. Hunger and a lack of sleep will make you feel more irritable.
5. **Use good coping mechanisms**: To improve resilience in the long term try engaging in positive coping mechanisms. Try your hand at a new hobby or interest.
6. **Avoid maladaptive coping mechanisms**: Things like alcohol, drugs or comfort eating have the potential to make you more miserable, feel guilty and act impulsively.
7. **Join an exercise plan or a sport:** When we exercise or play a sport, endorphins are released, which make us feel positive and confident. But start slow and try not to exert yourself at the beginning, as it might do more harm than good.
8. **Remind yourself of all the positive things**: Think of all the good things you have in your life. These could be achievements in school, a loving family and various career prospects.
9. **Use the experience as a learning curve:** Try and improve your response to certain challenges that you faced in your relationship or any shortcomings you thought you had.

10. **Seek professional help**: If you feel that you are struggling and are unable to cope, there are professional services available, including counsellors, psychologists and psychiatrists, to help you overcome this difficult time in your life.

When relationships break down, it is undoubtedly a difficult time for the person. It is natural for their family and friends to feel concerned. It is tough to see a loved one going through an emotionally turbulent time, especially when they don't want to acknowledge the hurt or seek help. But as well-wishers, we can surely do things that can help the person process the loss and move forward in a positive and healthy manner.

How to support someone going through a break-up:

1. Listen to them. Give them the space and time to vent their feelings.
2. Do not be judgemental; be supportive.
3. Try to engage them in relaxing or distracting activities that they like.
4. Provide practical assistance, like getting them class notes or running errands for them.
5. Avoid suggesting or encouraging the use of alcohol, drugs or cigarettes as a way of managing distress.
6. Be vigilant. Ask them to seek assistance or alert their family if there are any signs of suicidal thoughts.

Finally, it takes two to make or break a relationship. Carl Jung, a Swiss psychiatrist, famously said, 'The meeting of two personalities is like the contact of two chemical substances: if there is any reaction, both are transformed.' One hopes that there would be a positive change in both the persons, but this is not always the case. Meeting emotional needs is paramount in any relationship.

Each relationship serves a different purpose in our lives and teaches us something different. While the end of a relationship often feels like the end of the world, the reality of life is that we would go through many ups and downs in our lives and relationships. We can learn invaluable lessons in what to do and what not to do in relationships. The pace and pressures of modern life can demand all of one's attention, which can be used as a way to move on faster. However, this should not be used as an avoidance strategy. While the ideal goal would be to build long-lasting relationships, we can all learn to manage our break-ups better so that we grow to be wiser and more resilient as people.

KEY POINTS

1. Relationships are important in life.
2. Relationships are two-way streets and both sides have to work on them equally.
3. Our personalities are altered by our relationships and each relationship serves a different purpose in our lives.
4. It is okay to feel sad when a relationship breaks down but it is important to express this sadness and not bottle up emotions.
5. Give yourself the opportunity to accept and resolve the problem by not isolating yourself.
6. Seek help if you are struggling. Counselling, support groups and medication can help, depending on the intensity of symptoms.

4

SOCIAL MEDIA, SELF-ESTEEM AND SELF-CONFIDENCE

'Comparison is the thief of joy.'

—THEODORE ROOSEVELT

The use of social media is growing exponentially, and people across generations are using social media platforms in one way or the other. Human beings are social animals and like to stay connected with others. The virtual connection has become a significant, if not primary, form of contact these days.

It is said that addiction is opposite of connection.' When we are unable to connect with other people, or form meaningful relationships, we start looking for its equivalent in other things. We may choose to alleviate our loneliness with alcohol, gaming or social media.

We will be talking about alcohol use and addiction in a separate chapter of this book, but the CAGE questionnaire that is used to screen people for alcoholism, is relevant in this context.[2] It consists of four questions:

1. Have you ever felt that you should cut down on your alcohol use?
2. Have people annoyed you by criticizing your drinking?
3. Have you ever felt bad or guilty about your drinking?
4. Have you ever used alcohol as an eye-opener to steady your nerves in the morning?

Now, alter it to fit social media addiction:

1. Have you ever felt that you should cut down on your social media use?
2. Have parents/friends annoyed you by criticizing your excessive use of social media?
3. Have you ever felt bad or guilty for wasting time on social media?
4. Do you use your phone and check social media as soon as you open your eyes in the morning?

A 'yes' to two or more questions might suggest that it is an issue and you should think about changing your habits.

The pressing need to stay connected via the Internet, social media, television and news is increasingly taking the form of an addiction. People neglect other pleasures and important things in life, such as spending quality time with loved ones and studying.

---

[2] Ewing, J.A., 'Detecting Alcoholism The CAGE Questionnaire', *JAMA*, Vol. 252, No. 14, 1984, pp. 1905–07.

Social Media: A Double-Edged Sword

Anurag, a student of Class 8, would always feel lethargic during the day. During classes, he would usually doze off, get scolded by his teachers, perform poorly in academics and generally fail his exams. When his worried parents met his teachers about their growing concern about his rapidly falling grades, they realized that he was spending hours on social media. He was distracted and slept little at night. Only likes and comments on his posts would make him happy.

Social media can have positive and negative effects on a person. For people who are lonely or marginalized, social media can provide a platform to find like-minded individuals and help find sources of emotional support. It can give people comfort and connect them to other people facing similar problems.

But for a lot of users, social media tends to have negative effects. Social media can be thought of as a 'highlight reel' of somebody's life—it only serves to broadcast the positive aspects of a person's life, such as doing well at work, their holidays and their positive experiences, but it conveniently omits the challenges and negative fallouts in their life. Social media, therefore, can never be truly representative of real life. It is very carefully thought out and designed to give the best possible impression of a smooth-sailing life. Whatever people post about does not have to be genuine. Several 'filters' can alter people's appearances with a simple click. This can create a dissatisfaction with life and particularly cause unhappiness about how one looks. Furthermore, how others receive our pictures and the numbers of likes and shares on these pictures, alter our mood and confidence.

Jessica, a 19-year-old girl, is Internet-savvy and loves using social media. She is good with almost everything she does. She likes to stay connected with her friends and followers through social media. She, unfortunately, went through a break-up and was criticized by her boyfriend over the Internet.

Despite having thousands of connections, she felt incredibly lonely and embarrassed by the event, and got trolled. She started feeling anxious with every notification that popped up on her phone.

She eventually silenced the notifications from her social media accounts. She took a break from social media for a few months to maintain her sanity and lift her spirits.

Humans are given to comparison because, whether we like it or not, success is relative, and there is always someone who has more or is doing better than you. Social media makes comparing easier and gives it an unsavoury twist, whereby one overlooks all the positives in their life and wants what the other person has.

The need to feel wanted and accepted while also standing out from the crowd leads to people engaging in behaviours that are out of character—a tendency that social media is not only home to but also actively perpetuates. The excessive use of social media has been linked to increased loneliness, jealousy, anxiety, depression and reduced social skills.

Let me explain with an example. 'Fitspiration' is a concept that has come up from social media. According to the Oxford Dictionary, it is defined as, 'A person or thing that serves as motivation for someone to sustain or improve health and fitness.' This is done primarily through food and exercise. Although it is good to inspire people towards a healthier lifestyle, according to research, many students who were shown these pictures actually felt worse about their physical appearance, which negatively affected their body image and self-esteem.

Reetika is a 14-year-old who recently joined social media. She was overwhelmed by the presence of so many people across platforms and the extremely high beauty standards. Over time, she started comparing herself to people online, not knowing that people often manipulate their images. She began taking extreme measures to look like the people she saw on her phone and started using various filters to look 'better'. She felt stressed about her appearance all the time and took drastic measures to control her weight.

Self-Esteem and Self-Confidence

Self-esteem is a relatively new concept that refers to a person's overall sense of self-worth and their evaluation of themselves. Self-confidence is about your trust in your own abilities. Both terms are related, but the primary difference between them is that self-esteem is like the seasons of the year, whereas self-confidence is like the daily weather. It may be winter and it can rain, but there can still be sunny days. You may have good self-esteem, but there may be areas where you lack confidence. Self-confidence can be thought about in terms of external successes, while self-esteem is based on more internal matters.

The best way to understand self-esteem is perhaps by understanding Abraham Maslow's hierarchy of needs, as shown below.

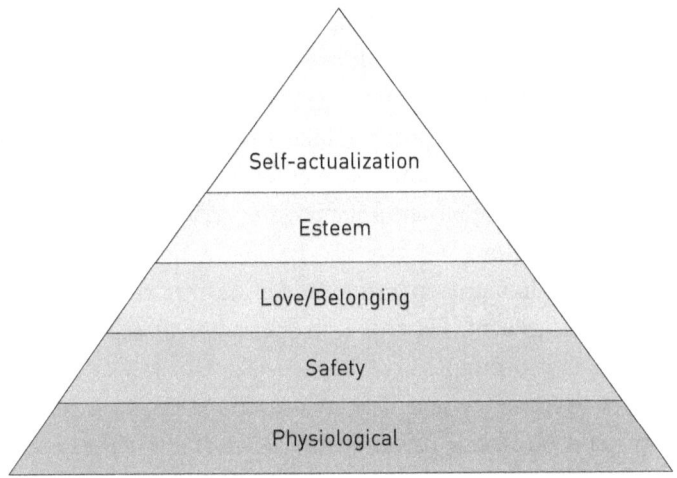

Figure 7: Abraham Maslow's Theory of Human Motivation

In this paper and his subsequent work, Maslow described a hierarchy of needs essential for human growth and development in the form of a pyramid where the most basic needs that need to be met first are at the bottom. As we move towards the top the needs reduce in order of urgency.

Physiological needs refer to the availability of basic necessities like water, food and shelter. The second level is safety, which means safeguarding one's personal and financial health, and being safe from accidents. 'Love and belonging' stands for love interests, sexual needs and belonging to certain social groups. 'Esteem' means being respected in society; this also includes fame, status and recognition. 'Self-actualization' stands for a person realizing their full potential and achieving what they can.

This order of needs, while relevant as a general rule of thumb, perhaps isn't the most accurate when it comes to the actual day-to-day living of the modern-day human, and especially the young adult. Most of our primary needs as depicted in the pyramid are generally taken care of by our families. Other priorities take their place, and often, a darker side of this pyramid can emerge if the need for love, belonging and esteem are not met.[3] An example of the same is illustrated below.

In the re-imagined pyramid, the most important and basic level is 'self-esteem'. Having a strong sense of self-esteem is essential as it promotes confidence. A lack of self-esteem can cause stress, anxiety and depression. The question is how do we try and boost our self-esteem? Increasingly, self-esteem is becoming linked to materialism and looking at and deriving pleasure from comments and likes from social media. Any negative comments or feeling neglected by others can shatter this fragile self-esteem.

The second level is that of feeling a sense of 'belonging'. This belonging comes from being part of 'high-end' or exclusive groups, which may include living in a particular area, driving a particular car, going on luxury holidays, and so on. This desire to belong may come at the cost of avoiding other essential things like one's health or relationships. One might also start living beyond their means and ultimately face financial and social struggles.

The third level is 'being connected', which is closely related to the two lower levels—the need or desire to go out and be connected to others at all times, the anxiety of missing a phone call or having to watch the latest film.

---

[3]Rastogi, Vipul, 'Time to Rethink Maslow's Hierarchy of Needs', *Time of India Blogs*, 2016, http://tinyurl.com/2xr5ckeb. Accessed on 3 January 2024.

The fourth and fifth levels are 'safety' and 'physiological' needs, but they are often not a personal priority, and are taken care of by our parents. While growing up we seldom realize that we would eventually need to meet these needs on our own.

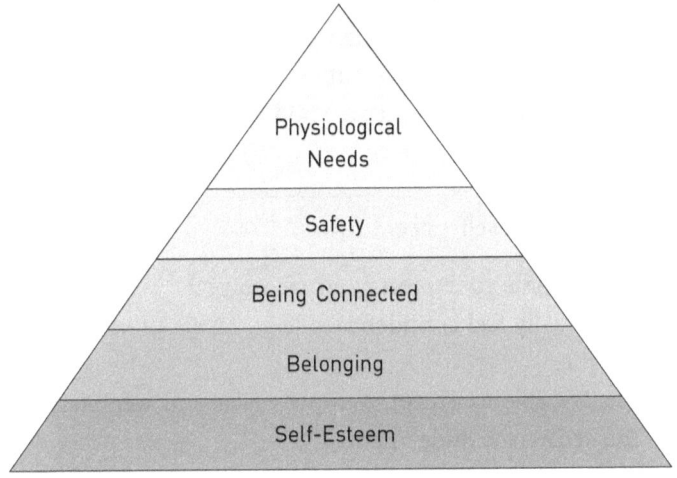

Figure 8: Example of a modified Theory of Human Motivation

The 'self-actualization' level from Maslow's original pyramid is often left unachieved because we set goals for our lives by measuring other people's success. There is always someone with better contacts, a bigger house, faster car or deeper pockets. There will always be two sides to this; the positive side is that people may actually go on to achieve more because they might be comparing themselves with people who have achieved more. The downside is that they will never be happy or satisfied with life when they have a frail ego and low self-esteem.

Self-esteem plays a significant role in one's motivation and eventual success. High self-esteem will give us that extra push to achieve things because the person perceives life positively and has believed in themselves; on the other hand, low self-esteem will hold a person back because they don't believe in themselves or feel capable of success.

Self-esteem is dependent on several things, including genetics, personality, upbringing, age, physical illnesses or physical limitations. Being subjected to excessive criticism from family and friends as a child can cause a lifetime of poor self-esteem.

Signs of healthy self-esteem levels:

1. You are able to express your needs.
2. You usually feel confident while going about your day-to-day life.
3. You are able to accept your strengths and weaknesses.
4. You trust your judgement.
5. You avoid dwelling on past events and use those experiences to improve and grow.
6. You have a positive outlook towards life.
7. You are assertive and can hold your ground when required.

Signs of low self-esteem levels:

1. You believe others are better than you.
2. You struggle to say 'no'.
3. You feel undeserving of praise.
4. You often have a negative outlook towards life.
5. You feel that you have low self-confidence.
6. You face difficulty in expressing your needs.
7. You have an intense fear of failure.

Ego

Ego is only slightly different from self-esteem. If self-esteem is about being assertive, ego is about being arrogant. In a way, it is how we perceive our connection with and importance to the outside world and people in our life. It is a loosely used term which is used to mean that a person is sensitive to criticism or setbacks.

Being egoistic can have some advantages too. The person can be more motivated to achieve their goals and be more willing to take risks. It can potentially lead to a lack of empathy, discourage others and ruin personal and professional relationships. The lack of self-reflection can hamper work and personal development.

Having high self-esteem can be a strength and blessing, as people with high self-esteem are generally self-sufficient, secure and, therefore, team players. An inflated self-esteem is, however, not good, as one comes across as self-centred and aggressive, which could potentially hamper relationships; similarly, an extremely low sense of self-esteem will affect your progress as you will go through life with an overwhelming experience of underachievement. A realistic yet positive view of oneself is considered ideal.

While self-esteem is an inherent quality, it can be modified. Improving your self-esteem starts by respecting yourself and being more self-aware and accepting. The constant feeling of comparing and fixing yourself is counterproductive, because this is a never-ending cycle.

Improving Self-Esteem

In his paper 'Alcoholism and Childhood', Dr G. Basil Price wrote, 'A nation's greatest asset is to be found in the well-being of its rising generation.'[4] This statement is very true for almost everything, including one's aspirations, health and education. The generation gap currently is more comprehensive than ever. With the largest percentage of population being under the age of thirty, it is important to ensure its well-being, which includes inculcating a healthy sense of self-esteem.

1. **Celebrate your hard work and achievements**: Be kind to yourself and reward yourself for your hard work.
2. **Learn something new**: Learning something new, such as a language or a musical instrument, can improve one's confidence and self-esteem exponentially.
3. **Reduce screen time**: More than an hour of television and/or mobile phone, regardless of what we watch, can cause lethargy, influence self-worth and increase procrastination.
4. **Take a break from social media**: This can help one step out of the cycle of over analysis and self-criticism.
5. **Stop being a perfectionist**: Set realistic targets. None of us can be good at everything; we all have our strengths and weaknesses.
6. **Help others**: Helping others makes us feel more capable and valuable. Volunteering is a good way of helping and giving something back to society.

---

[4]Price, G.B., 'Alcoholism and Childhood', *British Journal of Inebriety*, Vol. 8, No. 2, 1910, pp. 67–77.

Along with exercising moderation, the use of social media should be supplemented by the awareness that what we see on these platforms is only a selection of the best from the lives of others. This awareness would allow us to use social media in an inspirational way rather than causing unwanted comparison and low self-esteem. A healthy self-esteem will help you find the resilience to bounce back from failures in life and be more receptive to success.

KEY POINTS

1. Ego, self-esteem and self-confidence are related concepts.
2. Self-esteem can be low, high or inflated.
3. Being egoistical can have its advantages but there are many disadvantages, too.
4. Inflated ego can be a sign of narcissism.
5. It is important to focus on yourself and reflect on own well-being rather than compare yourself to more accomplished people.
6. Limiting social media use can save you time while also reducing irritability and helping maintain a healthy sense of self-esteem.

Part 2
HEALTH

'Your health is an investment, and not an expense.'

—JOHN QUELCH

5

WHAT IS ALL THE FUSS ABOUT SLEEP?

'If I don't sleep 11–12 hours per day, it's not right.'

—ROGER FEDERER

Put your finger down if you regularly think:

1. I need more sleep.
2. I waste my time mindlessly browsing social media.
3. I want to watch one more episode of this series before I sleep.
4. I wake up more tired than I felt before going to bed.
5. Sleep is a waste of time.
6. Sleeping fewer hours increases my efficiency and output.

Sleep is the most potent natural ability-enhancer available to human beings. Athletes like Roger Federer, Lebron James, Usain Bolt and Maria Sharapova famously sleep for about 10–12 hours a day. We might not have the luxury to sleep for so long, or indeed, need it. But a good night's sleep is essential to be able to function at your peak capacity.

Sleep is just as vital to our health as air, food, water and exercise. Unfortunately, sometimes, good sleep is hard to come by, and about 30–40 per cent of the population experiences some insomnia symptoms through the year.[5]

Insomnia

Insomnia is defined as dissatisfaction with sleep, both in terms of quality and quantity. There is no fixed amount of sleep that a person needs—anything around 7–8 hours is good.

Not all insomnias are concerning. People can experience transient insomnia, which most of us experience at some point in life. It normally occurs before exams or due to other acute stressors. Short-term insomnia can last for a few weeks. Chronic insomnia, the most worrying condition, can last several months or years.

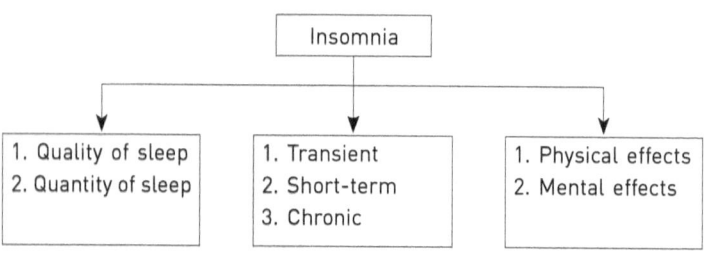

Figure 9: Different aspects of insomnia

---

[5]Roth, Thomas, 'Insomnia: Definition, Prevalence, Etiology, and Consequences', *Journal of Clinical Sleep Medicine*, Vol. 3, No. 5 suppl, August 2007, pp. S7–10.

The Dwindling Focus on Adequate Sleep

Sleep is 'restorative', that is, it helps our body build and repair muscles and tissues, ensures that our hormones perform optimally and helps us form strong, lasting memories. It is also 'preparative' as it gives us extra energy to be at our best the next day.

Unfortunately, the current pace of life is such that sleep is no longer a priority for us. Human beings as a species have been around for a long time and have evolved and adapted to life and changes in their environment. The pressure and stress that the current milieu presents is considerable, and it is exacerbated by lack of sleep. According to a survey, an average adult in the USA in the 1940s slept for about 7.9 hours every night, as compared to the current 6.8 hours.[6]

In about 70 years, we have given up on 15–20 per cent of our time dedicated to sleep. The loss of sleep time negatively impacts our health, causing heart diseases, diabetes and obesity. We all have the same 24 hours in the day, during which we face the pressure to work and achieve more. The easiest thing to sacrifice is sleep.

---

[6]Jones, Jeffrey M., 'In U.S., 40% Get Less than Recommended Amount of Sleep', *Gallup*, 19 December 2013, http://tinyurl.com/29hjt3c7. Accessed on 3 January 2024.

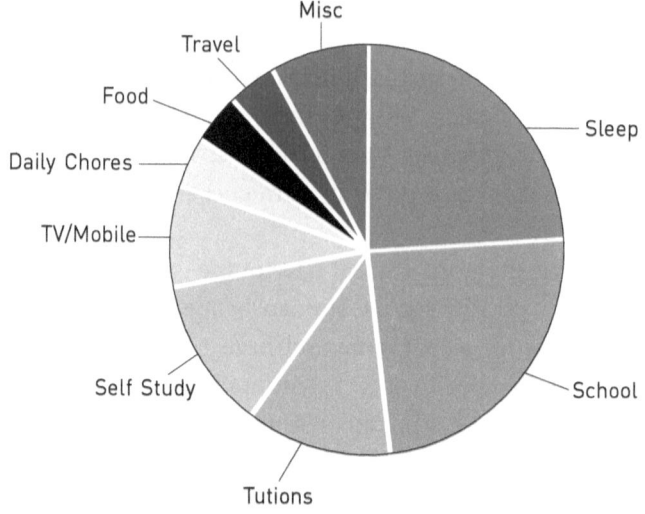

Figure 10: How an average adolescent spends their time

There is no perfect way to sleep. People in medieval times were said to follow polyphasic sleep patterns, which refers to sleeping in phases and not in one go.[7] There was a concept of first sleep and second sleep. People would sleep for four hours, then wake up to do some chores and then sleep again. In countries like Spain, people have a siesta during the day. But most of us sleep only at night.

Stress and Sleep

Stress and poor sleep are closely related and can form a vicious cycle.

---

[7]Gorvett, Zaria, 'The Forgotten Medieval Habit of "Two Sleeps"', *BBC*, 10 January 2022, http://tinyurl.com/yc2pvx39. Accessed on 3 January 2024.

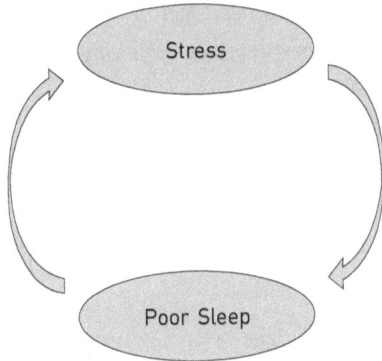

Figure 11: The vicious cycle of stress and bad sleep

Stress leads to poor sleep, and poor sleep increases stress. These days, we take pride in sleeping less and often boast that five or six hours of sleep is enough for us. And it is not just work or study pressures that make us lose sleep but also the desire to see one more episode of our favourite series or to complete another level of our video game.

It is not only the number of hours we sleep for that matters, but also the quality of sleep. Having a lot of tea, coffee and other energy or caffeine-based drinks alters sleep quality. This means that despite sleeping for a good number of hours, we can still wake up tired and drowsy because of poor sleep quality.

Amita is a student in her last year of graduate school. She has a lot going on, and she has not been able to make enough time during the day for her studies, college applications, preparations for graduation, etc. To manage everything simultaneously, she has been digging into her sleep hours and staying up late to finish her work for the last month. She has started consuming more coffee to stay awake.

Consequently, she has been feeling more irritable than usual and has noticed that she has been making more mistakes while studying.

It is a known fact that lack of sleep reduces alertness and is often the cause for accidents. Lack of enough good quality sleep adversely impacts our concentration, study and work performance, and we have to work harder and longer to achieve our goals and targets.

Good sleep requires two components to work in tandem—the body needs to be tired and the mind needs to be relaxed.

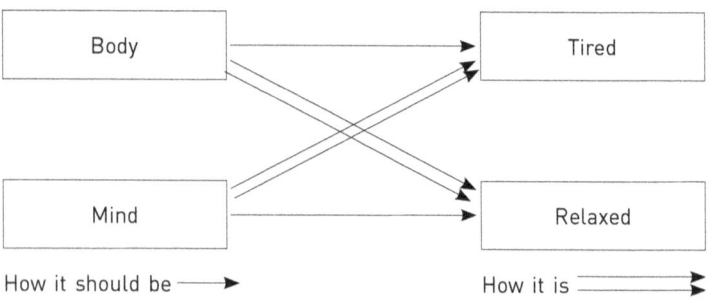

Figure 12: Mind–body balance for good sleep: what it should be versus what it is

Due to our sedentary lifestyles, people often find that while their bodies are relatively inactive, their minds are tired. This can lead to further frustration, and people can take extreme steps to get good quality sleep. Addictions are prevalent in scenarios where people start using alcohol and non-prescription drugs as ways to sleep better. The assumption that alcohol improves sleep is actually a myth because it, in actuality, spoils the sleep structure.[8]

---

[8]Ibid.

The lack of good sleep causes irritability, frustration and poor academic/professional performance. Difficulty sleeping can lead to anxiety and depressive disorders.

Therefore, compromising sleep in order to work or study for longer periods is a counterproductive strategy and affects our studies, relationships, health and work performance.

A note of caution: excess sleep could also point towards certain medical illnesses, but it more likely represents poor quality of sleep or avoidance behaviours (maladaptive coping). As with all things in life, it is crucial to strike a good balance.

KEY POINTS

Some tips for maintaining good sleep (sleep hygiene):

1. Try and maintain the same sleep routine, that is, waking up and sleeping at similar times.
2. Establish a good winding down routine before bed:
    - Switch off the television, put away your phone and/or computer an hour before bed. The light emitted from electronic devices serves to increase the alertness of our brains.
    - Read a light book or listen to relaxing music.
    - Write down your chores for the next day.
    - Dim the lights in the bedroom and preferably use yellow light with lamps pointing down.
3. Avoid caffeinated drinks after 5 p.m.
4. Try an hour of sports/exercises or hobbies in the daytime.
5. Only use your bed for sleeping at night. Do not watch television or study in bed.
6. Anything around 7–8 hours of sleep is sufficient for most of us.

6

NUTRITION FOR ADOLESCENTS

*'Food can be the greatest medicine,
or the slowest form of poison.'*

—ANN WIGMORE

We all want to be the fittest version of ourselves so that we look and feel better. Fitness doesn't just refer to physical fitness, but also represents a positive attitude towards life and makes you feel more confident about yourself.

Nutrition is defined as the scientific study of food and its relation to health. Our body needs 'optimal' nutrition, which means that a person should get all the essential nutrients in the correct proportions necessary for the body, while also creating a 'reserve' for times when we work out extra or for the future, when nutrition supply may be inadequate.

During adolescence, physical and psychological changes place a great demand on the body for macro and micronutrients.[9] Macronutrients are defined as nutrients

---

[9]Lassi, Zohra, Anoosh Moin and Zulfiqar Bhutta, 'Nutrition in Middle

required by our body in large amounts, such as carbohydrates, proteins and fats. Micronutrients, such as vitamins and minerals, are also essential but are required in lesser amounts.

Many young people in developing countries enter adolescence undernourished, while others have a good but unbalanced diet. This makes them more vulnerable to lifestyle-related diseases later in life. Therefore, inculcating adequate nutrition, eating healthy and engaging in physical exercise at this age are fundamental for good health in adulthood. So, to maintain good health in the future, one needs to understand the fundamentals of a balanced diet and follow it.

Our body is constantly working, even if we are sitting or lying down. A human adult has more than 10 trillion cells that work around the clock. Your heart, brain, immune system and kidneys, among other organs, are always at work, and they need proper nutrition to function adequately. Sometimes, we use calories as a way of judging nutritional requirements. A healthy adult male uses about 2,500 calories and a healthy adult woman uses about 2,000 calories.

The ICMR-National Institute of Nutrition, India, recommends sourcing macronutrients and micronutrients from a minimum of eight food groups per day. An exchange list contains a group of foods in specified amounts with approximately equal carbohydrate, protein and fat values. It also provides detailed information on nutrients for all the foods and beverages.

Childhood and Adolescence', *Child and Adolescent Health and Development*, Bundy Dap, Silva N.D., Horton S., et al. (eds), The International Bank for Reconstruction and Development, The World Bank, 2017.

> *An average diet should include*
>
> 1. Milk and milk products: 2 portions per day
> 2. Pulses and legumes: 2 portions per day
> 3. Meat, fish and poultry: 1 portion per day
> 4. Fruits: 2 portions per day
> 5. Cereal: 6 to 12 portions per day
> 6. Fat exchange: 3 to 4 portions per day

Food exchange lists are used in meal planning to calculate the meals' energy, carbohydrate, fat and protein content.

We can also follow the plate method to design breakfast, lunch and dinner.

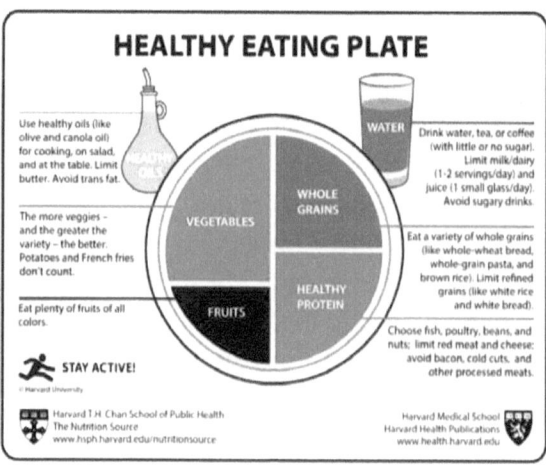

Figure 13: What a balanced plate looks like[10]

---

[10] Healthy Eating Plate, *The Nutrition Source*, Harvard T.H. Chan School of Public Health, 2011.

Most of us have a basic understanding of food components. But to understand the percentage of carbohydrates, proteins and fats that are essential to our meal plan, we first need to discuss the different roles they play in our body.

Carbohydrates

Most people associate carbohydrates with sugar. However, different types of carbohydrates serve different purposes for our bodies. Glucose is the most common form of carbohydrate, which stores and releases energy.

The glycaemic index (GI) is a parameter that can help you assess if a carbohydrate is good for you or not. GI is the value assigned to specific foods in the range of 0–100 that shows how fast a food can cause a person's blood sugar to rise. Foods with lower GI are preferable.

In the glycaemic index, foods are classified under the following categories:

a. Low GI: 55 or less
b. Medium GI: 56–69
c. High GI: 70 and above

Some examples of very low GI foods include meat, fish (tuna, mackerel, salmon), poultry, oils (olive, coconut), vegetables, herbs (turmeric, cinnamon, black pepper, cumin), nuts (almond, walnut, pistachios) and seeds (chia, flax, sesame).

Some examples of low GI foods are whole grains, legumes, fruits and non-starchy vegetables.

Some examples of high GI foods are bread, rice, bakery products, cereals, pasta, noodles, starchy vegetables, sugar-sweetened beverages, snacks like microwave popcorn, chips, chocolates, crackers, and so on.

Carbohydrates can be further divided into two main types.

1. Simple carbohydrates: These are made up of just one or two sugar units. Some familiar simple carbohydrate sources are milk, fruits and dairy products. Processed and refined sugars are found in sweets, syrups, processed juices, table sugar and carbonated beverages. They are easily digestible and an instant source of energy.
2. Complex carbohydrate: These are made up of multiple sugar molecules joined together in long chains. Complex carbohydrates can be found in foods such as peas, beans, whole grains and vegetables. They provide a more sustained release of energy.

All carbohydrates are turned into glucose in the body and are used as energy.

Role of carbohydrates in our body:

- Carbohydrates provide a fast source of energy. They spare proteins so that the latter can be used to build and repair tissues and muscles.
- Lactose encourages the growth of favourable intestinal bacteria and enhances the absorption of calcium.
- Glucose alone works as a source of energy for the central nervous system.
- Cellulose provides faecal bulk, which helps bowel movement.

Excess of carbohydrates in the diet, mainly sucrose (table sugar), increases the incidence of dental caries, causes obesity and irritates the gastrointestinal tract. It also increases the blood triglycerides and cholesterol levels, leading to an increased prevalence of heart disease.

Our diet should include complex carbohydrates if we want to increase our energy levels. These could include bran chapatti, oatmeal, brown rice, brown bread and whole wheat pasta.

Adolescents should avoid simple carbohydrates or sugar-rich food like white bread, processed foods, sweets or foods with a high glycaemic index, as they can increase the chances of obesity.

Proteins

Protein is a macronutrient that is essential for building muscle mass. Proteins are the fundamental components of living cells and are made of carbon, oxygen, nitrogen and hydrogen in different proportions. Almost half of the protein in our body is muscles, and the other half is present in the form of bone, cartilage and skin. Proteins, which have various functions in the body, also provide energy.

Amino acids are required to make proteins, and, therefore, exercise enthusiasts take amino acid supplements to build muscles. They are further classified into two groups: essential amino acids, which have to be consumed through diet as they are not synthesized within the human body, and non-essential amino acids, which can be synthesized within the body.

The requirement of protein per person varies according to age, physical activity and stress. Infants, children, pregnant women and people with infections or illnesses require more protein. Rich protein sources are milk, meat, fish, eggs and plant foods like pulses and legumes. Animal bodies are more similar to human bodies and, therefore, animal proteins are considered to be of higher quality as they provide all the essential amino acids in the correct proportions. In contrast, plant or vegetable proteins are considered somewhat inferior as they can be low on some essential amino acids. However, the notion that a vegan diet, one that is devoid of all animal products, cannot be balanced, is misguided. A combination of a variety of cereals, millets and pulses can provide all the protein necessary for our bodies.

Adolescents need more protein intake to increase their muscle mass. So, it is advisable to take high biological value (HBV) protein from sources like eggs, chicken and seafood (salmon, tuna, prawn, shrimp). Athletes may need more protein compared to non-athletic adolescents.

An adolescent's diet can also include vegetable protein sources like soybean, tofu, paneer, quinoa and amaranth.

Fats

There are two main sources of dietary fats: the invisible fats present in plant and animal foods, and the visible fats that are added during the preparation of food. Fats are also vehicles for fat-soluble vitamins, like vitamins A, D, E, K and beta carotenes, and aid in their absorption. They are sources of essential polyunsaturated fatty acids which reduce the level of bad cholesterol. It is crucial to have adequate and good quality fat in one's diet with sufficient polyunsaturated fatty acids in proper proportions for the body to meet the essential fatty acid requirement. The quality and type of fat in the diet impacts cholesterol and triglyceride levels in the blood.

A healthy and balanced diet for adolescents should include an adequate amount of fat to provide concentrated energy since their energy needs per kilogram of body weight are nearly twice as those of adults. Adults should restrict excessive saturated fats (butter, ghee and hydrogenated fats) and cholesterol (red meat). An excess of saturated fats can cause obesity, diabetes, cardiovascular disease and cancer.

Healthy fats are found in nuts (almonds, walnuts), avocado and peanut butter. These foods should be consumed regularly by adolescent girls and boys. Intake of the right amounts and types of fat is one way to reduce the risk of diseases and improve your overall health and quality of life.

Vitamins and Minerals

Vitamins are the chemical compounds that are required by the body in small proportions. They should be taken through the foods in the diet as they are not synthesized in our bodies. Vitamins help body processes as well as aid in the maintenance of skin, bones, nerves, blood, eyes and brain. They can be classified into two types: fat soluble (vitamins A, D, E, and K) and water soluble (vitamin C and the B-complex vitamins like thiamine, pyridoxine, folic acid and cyanocobalamin, among others). Some pro-vitamins such as beta-carotene is converted to vitamin A in the body. The fat-soluble vitamins can be stored in the body, while water-soluble vitamins get excreted in the urine. The B-complex vitamins and Vitamin C are easily destroyed by exposure to heat or air during cooking and food processing. Hence, eating fresh and raw foods like salads and fruits is essential for our body.

Minerals are inorganic elements/metals that are found in body tissues. The major macro minerals are sodium, calcium, phosphorous, potassium, magnesium and sulphur, while zinc, copper, cobalt, fluorine, molybdenum, chromium and iodine are micro minerals. Their role is to maintain the integrity of skin, hair, nails, blood and soft tissues. They also help in nerve impluse transmission.

An unhealthy, unbalanced diet and a tendency to skip meals can disturb hormonal levels and cause vitamin and mineral deficiencies. Vitamin D, folic acid and iron deficiencies are quite common in adolescent girls and should be regularly tested.

The aim of a balanced diet is to provide all the nutrients in proper proportions. You can easily accomplish this by consuming the right quantities of the four primary food groups. The body's nutrient requirement will vary according to the person's age, gender, any illnesses and levels of physical activity.

A Balanced Diet

A balanced diet should provide around:

- 50–60 per cent of total calories from carbohydrates, preferably from complex carbohydrates.
- 10–15 per cent of calories from proteins.
- 20–30 per cent of calories from both visible and invisible fat.

In addition, a balanced diet should provide other non-nutrients such as dietary fibre, antioxidants and phytochemicals. Antioxidants such as vitamins C and E, beta-carotene, riboflavin and selenium protect the human body from free radical damage. Other phytochemicals such as polyphenols, flavones, etc., also afford protection against oxidant damage. Spices like turmeric, ginger, garlic, cumin and cloves are rich in antioxidants. Free radicals and oxidants are chemical compounds that cause cellular damage and are linked to various body diseases.

Cooking

Learning to cook for yourself is an excellent way to manage your diet. The young adults of today are often called 'global citizens', with many vying to move abroad for further studies or for work. Learning to cook is not just a hobby but an essential life skill that each and every individual must have. Also, knowing what ingredients go into our food gives us better control and idea of what we eat, making diet management easier. It is best to start learning to cook early in life rather than waiting for the time to come to move out of your own home.

Some dishes are easy to master. They are easily made without much effort and provide adequate nutrition. When hungry, adolescents can fix their own food. They should explore easy and healthy options like:

1. Whole fruits
2. Fruit salads with various seeds and nuts (chia/flax/sunflower)
3. Roasted nuts
4. Omelette/boiled eggs
5. Vegetable, egg or meat sandwiches
6. Unsweetened cereal with milk and nuts
7. Fruit smoothies
8. Roasted cottage cheese with vegetables
9. Roasted/Grilled chicken
10. Sauteed vegetables

11. Vegetable or meat rolls
12. Baked chicken nuggets
13. Vegetable, lentil or chicken soup

Organic Foods

Organic foods are grown naturally by using natural manure or compost and without any synthetic chemicals or pesticides. Organic food is considered safer, healthier and is often tastier. It's safer for the environment and for the well-being of animals.

Organic meat, dairy and eggs are produced by livestock that only consumes organic, hormone-free and non-genetically modified diets. Natural methods are used for the prevention of diseases, and the livestock is not exposed to antibiotics. Livestock grows at their own pace with no artificial growth hormones being given to them.

Diet- and Lifestyle-Related Diseases

Lifestyle diseases are non-communicable diseases associated with having a poor lifestyle and based on having poor day-to-day habits. These are diseases that are primarily caused or compounded by stress, very little physical activity, poor diet and/or the use of substances like cigarettes and alcohol.

1. **Hypothyroidism:** Also called underactive thyroid disease, this slows down the body's metabolism. It is often characterized by sudden weight gain/obesity, feeling sluggish, hair-fall, low Vitamin B12 and Vitamin D3 levels, increased water retention, menstrual irregularities and bloating. A healthy,

nutritious diet can be very helpful in balancing the hormonal changes along with medication.

2. **PCOS/PCOD (polycystic ovarian syndrome/disorder):** This lifestyle disorder, which affects the ovaries, is becoming more common these days, both in teenagers and adults. PCOD is characterized by irregular periods, bloating and tiredness, mood swings, infertility, acne, excessive facial hair and weight gain. Symptoms can be controlled through lifestyle changes, maintaining a healthy weight and eating a balanced diet with all essential nutrients.

3. **Bulimia nervosa:** This is a common severe eating disorder usually seen among adolescents. People with bulimia tend to binge eat large amounts of food and then make themselves vomit to compensate for eating that much. It is characterized by a preoccupation with the fear of gaining weight, and repeated episodes of eating abnormally large amounts of food in one sitting. Effective treatment can be carried out via psychological help from a professional, along with a better understanding of food.

4. **Anorexia nervosa:** This is another prevalent eating disorder characterized by a distorted body image, with a phobia of being overweight. Patients reduce their caloric intake significantly to prevent weight gain and further manage weight by increasing exercise, inducing vomit or using weight-loss pills.

Anorexia, like other eating disorders, is very debilitating and can be extremely difficult to manage. It can be helped by adopting a healthy lifestyle, better eating habits and comprehensive psychological support.

5. **Diabetes:** It is a chronic non-communicable disorder that affects how food gets converted into energy inside the body. There are two types of diabetes:
   - Type 1: It is also known as insulin-dependent or juvenile or childhood-onset diabetes. The body cannot produce the required amount of insulin, and therefore, it must be supplemented externally. Generally, it is found in children, teens and young adults.
   - Type 2: It is known as non-insulin-dependent or adult-onset diabetes. In this, the body cannot use insulin in the body to maintain blood sugar levels. It can be prevented by a healthy lifestyle, such as being physically active, eating healthy food and maintaining a healthy body weight. Foods with low GI can help manage blood glucose levels.
6. **Hypertension:** This is another relatively common chronic lifestyle disease where the blood pressure is high. This can lead to headaches, heart diseases and brain strokes. A low-calorie, low-fat and low-salt diet is prescribed, with normal protein intake. Try and eat fresh food and avoid preserved, canned and pickled food as they are likely to have extra salt in them, to prevent hypertension later in life. Some salad dressings also have a high sodium content and therefore should be avoided.
7. **Obesity:** The World Health Organisation (WHO) has defined obesity as having excessive fat that may impair health. Body mass index (BMI) is a common method that can be used to measure obesity in adults. It is calculated by dividing a person's weight in kilograms

by the square of their height in metres (kg/m^2).

Obesity is currently considered a pandemic, and over 340 million children and adolescents aged between 5–19 were found to be overweight or obese in 2016.[11]

Raised BMI will cause other non-communicable diseases like diabetes, hypertension, cardiovascular disease, osteoarthritis, etc. It is essential to try and live an active life from childhood while consuming a balanced and healthy diet. This reduces the likelihood of developing the above-mentioned chronic diseases.

8. **Acne:** More commonly known as pimples, this can be a chronic condition that affects more than 85 per cent of adolescents and two-thirds of adults aged 18 years and older.[12]

It is a skin condition where dead skin and sebum—natural oil produced by the skin—clog hair follicles, causing the appearance of blackheads, whiteheads and pimples. It is traditionally considered more common in adolescents though it affects all ages. It happens as hormonal changes occur in the body after puberty.

Research studies have shown that diet plays a crucial role in controlling acne. Some foods increase blood sugar quickly, causing insulin to be released into the blood. Insulin can impact oil glands and produce more oil which will increase the risk of acne. Therefore,

---

[11] 'Obesity and Overweight', *World Health Organization*, 9 June 2021, http://tinyurl.com/bdbfy5dd. Accessed on 3 January 2024.

[12] Alanazi, Manal Saeed, et al., 'Prevalence and Psychological Impact of Acne Vulgaris among Female Secondary School Students in Arar City, Saudi Arabia, in 2018', *Electronic Physician*, Vol. 10, No. 8, 2018, pp. 7224–29, http://tinyurl.com/ywfekjt8. Accessed on 3 January 2024.

it is advised to have a protein-rich and low GI diet. Safe foods include unprocessed fruits, vegetables, whole grains, legumes, nuts, fish and seeds.

Avoid foods with high sugar content, like chocolates, fried foods and dairy products.

Foods That Boost Immunity

Immunity is the mechanism that enables our body to fight diseases. There are three types of immunity:

1. **Innate:** It is the natural immunity everyone is born with.
2. **Active:** It is also called adaptive immunity. It is developed throughout an individual's life through vaccines or when one is exposed to a disease.
3. **Passive:** This is taken from another source and is temporary. In this particular type of immunity, antibodies for a disease are taken from one individual and given to one who has to combat it.

Every individual can do more to improve their immunity levels. The pillars of a healthy immune system can be described in the following way:

1. Eating a balanced diet means having all the nutrients in adequate proportions. The focus should be on fibres, protein, vitamin C, vitamin D and zinc.
2. Exercise daily for at least 45–60 minutes to strengthen the immune system.
3. Drink an adequate amount of water daily, which is about 8–10 glasses (2 litres), to keep the body hydrated and functioning properly.

4. Limit stress to the body. Set time aside for yourself. Keep your mind calm, engage in hobbies, talk to people you are close to, meditate, play games, read books, etc.
5. Eat a plate of colourful fruits and vegetables daily; also, include probiotic foods or drinks in your diet. Probiotics provide good bacteria to improve gut health, promote digestion and enhance immunity.
6. Avoid smoking and drinking as it can deteriorate the immunity-building cells.

Superfoods and Immunity

We all want to stay healthy and disease-free. Diet, exercise and having a good routine, all help in maintaining good health. 'Superfoods' is the term given to foods that are nutritionally dense, especially in antioxidants, vitamins and minerals.

The following food items are considered superfoods, which means that they are packed with more nutrients and are essential for our body to develop natural immunity. Whenever the season changes, many people catch the flu, but many others are unaffected because they have better immunity. Everyone should try to incorporate more of these food items in their diet in various ways to enhance immunity.

1. Citrus fruits: oranges, lemon, Indian gooseberry
2. Berries: strawberry, blueberry, blackberry
3. Nuts: almond, walnut
4. Seeds: chia, pumpkin, flax, sunflower
5. Curd/Yogurt
6. Ginger

7. Garlic
8. Turmeric
9. Red bell pepper
10. Cruciferous vegetables: broccoli, sprouts, cabbage
11. Fruits: papaya, kiwi
12. Tea: green, black
13. Fish: shellfish, salmon, tuna
14. Green leafy: spinach, mint, microgreens

Role of Parents

Improving adolescents' nutritional understanding and habits is an investment in their health. Allowing them to work with food and answering their questions is very important. Parents and schools should encourage food preparation, cooking classes and debates around food and dietary habits to increase awareness and help prevent severe and chronic lifestyle conditions in the future.

TIPS FOR PARENTS

1. Parents and family are the first role models for children. Encourage and help them develop healthier food habits.
2. Parents should be aware of the healthy and nutritionally dense foods that are available to them.
3. Parents should teach children about food and inculcate good eating habits from childhood.
4. Use rewards of fruits/vegetables/nutrient-dense sweets to praise the child's behaviour or activity.
5. Eating processed or junk food sometimes is okay, but the majority of the child's diet should be home-cooked fresh food.
6. There should be no separate cooking for the child in general unless there are any specific health conditions.

7. Encourage the whole family to eat together.
8. Children should be advised about the impact of high fat, sugar, salt and processed food on their health.
9. Fruits and vegetables of all colours should be included in the diet, with a special focus on seasonal, locally produced and fresh food.

In summary, food and its fundamental understanding is essential for all. A famous saying goes, 'Let food be thy medicine.' If you eat good food, it will also work as medicine for your body and keep you healthy. The transition from adolescence to adulthood is crucial and will have a long-lasting impact on an individual's health; therefore, taking ownership of your health is essential.

SOME KEY POINTS

1. Eat three regular meals a day with some healthy snacks in between.
2. Increase fibre intake.
3. Reduce salt intake.
4. Eat balanced meals.
5. Eat fruits for snacks.
6. Drink adequate water during the day. (Fruit juices have a lot of calories and sometimes have added sugar. Whole fruit, therefore, is always a better choice.)
7. When cooking, try to bake or boil instead of frying.
8. Try and eat more chicken and fish rather than red meat, and choose lean cuts when possible.
9. Eat home-cooked meals as much as possible.
10. Purchase only a few soft drinks and high-fat snacks like chips, cookies and chocolates, and consume them occasionally.

7

PHYSICAL FITNESS, EXERCISE AND SUPPLEMENTS

'Inner fire is the most important thing that mankind possesses.'

—EDITH SÖDERGRAN

Kabir is a 16-year-old boy who idolizes Dwayne 'The Rock' Johnson. He wanted to bulk up and started training. He started following personal trainers on Instagram and eventually enrolled in a gym. He felt quite out of place as he didn't know which machines to use or how to use them. He was befriended by another gym member who advised him to start taking whey protein, BCAA and anabolic steroids to build bulk quickly.

He began experiencing hot flushes every day, and after three months, his kidney function started getting affected.

The notion that exercise is as important as medicine is quite prevalent, and there is an ever-growing awareness of the benefits of exercise. Do you think that's true?

Yes, exercise truly works as a medicine for our body. It is both preventive and restorative, that is, it prevents illnesses and helps restore previous body functions after diseases or injuries.

There is strong and growing evidence that physical activity plays a vital role in preventing and treating multiple disorders as well as promoting good health and well-being. Exercise is one prescription that could prevent and help treat dozens of diseases, such as diabetes, hypertension and obesity, and could also be tailored to an individual's needs.

Despite well-known health benefits, lack of physical activity is a pandemic affecting 25 per cent of adults globally.[13] Prolonged periods of sitting and other sedentary behaviours are associated with harmful health effects. Recent studies have demonstrated that more than 50 per cent of the average person's waking time involves prolonged sitting, such as with television viewing and computer use.[14]

What Is Physical Activity?

First, let's understand the concept of physical activity, exercise and physical fitness. Physical activity and physical exercise are terms that are often used interchangeably. All of us undertake some form of physical activity daily, but it does not necessarily mean that we have exercised. We exercise to achieve physical fitness. As per the WHO, 'physical activity' should not be confused with 'exercise', which is a subcategory of physical

---

[13]'Physical Activity', *World Health Organization*, 2020, http://tinyurl.com/a7c7bu52. Accessed on 3 January 2024.

[14]'World Health Organization Definition of Physical Activity', *Public Health Nigeria*, 2020, http://tinyurl.com/y7xctmp7. Accessed on 3 January 2024.

activity that is planned, structured, repetitive and aims to improve or maintain one or more components of physical fitness.

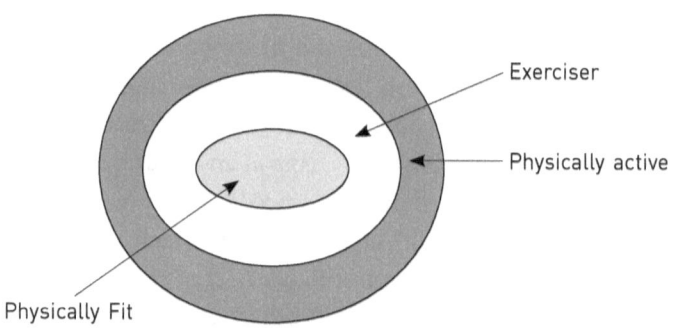

Figure 14: The difference between exercise, physical activity and being physically fit

Physical fitness is a person's ability to perform physical activity. The fitter you are, the better your ability to perform a physical activity. The majority of people might consider themselves physically fit if they can do the physical activities required at their work or other leisure activities. But that's not always true.

To be physically fit, each of the following health standards should be met:

1. **Cardiovascular endurance:** This is the heart and lungs' ability to supply oxygen during prolonged physical activity.
2. **Muscular endurance and strength:** This is the muscles' ability to perform without fatigue and with the adequate force needed to do the job.
3. **Healthy body composition:** This is the relative amount of body fat, muscle, bone mass and flexibility.

One should also be agile and have appropriate power, coordination, balance, quick reaction time and speed.

In a nutshell, a physically fit individual should be able to do daily tasks with vigour, alertness and accuracy without undue fatigue. At the same time, they should have the energy to enjoy leisure time and be able to meet unforeseen emergencies.

The Health Benefits of Exercise and Being Physically Fit

Medical studies emphasize that some exercise is better than none and more activity (up to a point) is better than less.

A workout session of 30 minutes can increase life expectancy by up to 3.7 years, while also improving the quality of life.[15] This alone should be a good enough reason to be active. A physically active child is more likely to become a physically active adult.

Physical activity decreases the risk of heart diseases, reduces cholesterol and blood pressure. It protects against certain cancers and can help prevent diabetes and aid in its treatment. Exercising regularly also encourages a person to have a healthier lifestyle, including having better eating habits and avoiding addictions. Last but not least, there is the psychological benefit of reduced stress, anxiety and depression. Being physically active also helps in weight management.

---

[15]Reimers, C.D., et al., 'Does Physical Activity Increase Life Expectancy? A Review of the Literature', *Journal of Aging Research*, Vol. 2012, pp. 1–9, http://tinyurl.com/3x7fsjud. Accessed on 3 January 2024.

What Should You Do if You Are Physically Active, but Not Physically Fit?

Even if you have a very sedentary lifestyle, nothing is lost. There is no better time to start looking after yourself than the present. The health benefits of starting the process of becoming physically fit are almost immediate.

If you wish to start, start low and go slow. Begin with a short and low-intensity activity and increase gradually. Start with walking for five to ten minutes each day, stretching, gardening or even playing with your dog. Any form of physical activity counts, and the more you do, the better you become.

How Should One Start an Exercise Programme?

Anyone can start exercising, but it's always good to be safe. Someone without any health issues can begin at a low intensity and gradually build from there. You should work on volume and consistency before intensity and make progress in small increments towards your goal. This allows your body time to adapt to the increased training load and prevent injuries that can happen from doing too much too fast. If there is a question or concern, talking to your doctor is advisable. It is also a good practice to self-screen before choosing and starting an exercise program.

There are self-assessment tools to guide pre-participation evaluation. Two self-screening tools that can be used are the Physical Activity Readiness Questionnaire (PAR-Q) and the American Heart Association/American College of Sports Medicine Pre-participation Questionnaire (AAPQ). Risk assessment is done based on the answers, and these tests can guide us if we need to see a doctor before starting physical exercise.

In general, exercise does not provoke adverse heart-related events in a healthy individual with normal heart and lungs.

Adequate warm-up, stretching and cool-down techniques can prevent musculoskeletal injuries related to overuse and sprains/strains. It is always advisable to have a coach/guide when starting new exercise regimens, especially when they are high-intensity workouts.

How Much Exercise Should One Undertake?

Our body burns energy all the time. One way to calculate your body's energy expenditure is by calculating metabolic equivalents (METs), which show your working metabolic rate ratio relative to your resting metabolic rate. Metabolic rate is the rate of energy used by the body per unit of time. It is one way to describe the intensity of an exercise or activity.

MET = Working Metabolic Rate/Resting Metabolic Rate

In simple terms, five METs mean that you are working five times harder than you would be when you are at rest.

Light intensity exercise uses from 1.6 to 3.0 METs. Examples are walking at a leisurely pace or standing in line at the store.

Moderate intensity uses from 3.0 to 6.0 METs. Examples include taking a brisk walk, swimming slowly or cycling on level ground.

Vigorous intensity exercise uses 6 METs or more. On a scale relative to an individual's capacity, vigorous-intensity physical activity is usually a 7 or 8 on a scale of 0–10. Examples include running, playing a sport or cycling up a steep hill.

For children and adolescents who have no chronic health conditions, the WHO recommends 60 minutes or more of physical activity every day. The physical activity should include moderate to vigorous intensity aerobic physical activity three days a week along with muscle and bone-strengthening activities three days a week.

For adults aged 18 to 64 without any chronic conditions, 150 minutes (30 minutes daily for five days per week) of moderate-intensity or 75 minutes of vigorous-intensity aerobic activity per week is recommended. Adults should undertake muscle-strengthening activity two or more days per week.

Aerobic activities, also called endurance activities, are activities that improve cardiorespiratory fitness. Examples of aerobic exercises include brisk walking, running, bicycling, jumping rope and swimming.

Components of a good exercise programme:

- Aerobic (500 to 1000 METS/week): If you do a 30-minute brisk walk five days a week, you are doing around 750 METS/week.
- Resistance (two to three days/week): Train each major muscle group. At least 48 hours should separate the exercise training session for the same muscle groups.
- Flexibility (two to three times/week): Otherwise known as stretching, this should be performed after exercising as it acutely impacts power and strength.
- Neuromotor exercise training (two to three times/week): Also called as functional training, this exercise group focusses on balance, agility, coordination and gait.

Perceived Barriers to Exercising

Most people know that exercise will help them improve their physical and mental health, but unfortunately, they find it difficult to get started. This could be because of many reasons that are listed below, along with tips on overcoming them:

- Time constraints: You can break sessions into blocks and incorporate exercise as you go about your day making different choices, such as taking the stairs instead of the elevator.
- Monotony: Exercising with a friend, involving your family, adding a variety of exercises or sports, having equipment at home, watching the news or games or listening to music while exercising can help alleviate the monotony.
- Joining a gym is expensive: You can save money by exercising or taking walks outside, following along to exercise videos at home and taking the stairs more frequently.
- Not enough knowledge: Ask for guidance from a trainer at your local gym or sports centre.

It is important to note that the best physical activity is the one you enjoy. It should not feel like a burden or homework because that will be unsustainable in the long run.

A Few More Tips

Everyone should expect a net health benefit by exercising. Choose an enjoyable activity where one feels competent and safe. It should be readily accessible and should fit easily into one's daily schedule. It should be cost-effective and not cause an unnecessary financial burden. Choose to exercise with a friend for better long-term sustainability of the exercise program.

As a jumping-off point, aim for 30 minutes of moderate physical activity for at least five days, or a total of 150 minutes a week. In fact, you may start with a few minutes a day and increase your workout time slowly by 5–10 minutes every week until you achieve your target.

If walking is not your cup of tea, you can consider other moderate-intensity exercises, like swimming, stair-climbing, tennis or dancing. Don't forget that household activities can count as well, such as mopping the floor, gardening or anything that gets you to break out in a light sweat.

Yoga

Let's talk about yoga. It is one of several mind-and-body practices that use interactions among the mind, body and behaviour to promote health. There are three components of yoga:

1. Postures (*āsanas*): These help increase flexibility and improve balance.
2. Breath control/regulated breathing (*prānāyāma*): This is a form of meditation in itself that focusses on breath control.
3. Meditation (*dhyāna*): Helps in focussing and clearing the mind. It may include chanting.

Yoga improves strength, flexibility and balance, but it does not necessarily improve aerobic fitness. It helps reduce blood pressure, stress, anxiety and depression. It is very helpful in managing lower back pain and other painful conditions as a supplement to medications.[16] Many people also practise yoga for spiritual reasons.

Yoga is relatively risk-free, but there is a potential risk of musculoskeletal injuries, most commonly hamstring and knee injuries. Overall, yoga is a safe low- to moderate-exertion exercise.

Nutrition

Nutrition is a science that interprets the nutrients and energy in food. Optimal nutrition allows you to stay healthy and maximizes sports training and performance. Optimal nutrition allows you to have enough energy to go through your day and maximizes your performance in exercise and sports.

Carbohydrates are fuel for moderate to intense exercises. Before exercising, one can load up on muscle carbohydrate stores and include a small amount of protein in a pre-exercise meal or snack for building and repairing muscle tissue. The intake of protein before exercising may help reduce post-exercise muscle soreness. Choose a pre-exercise meal that is low in fat and fibre.

Hydration is essential while exercising, and the fluid lost through sweat should be replenished. There can be consequences of excessive (more than two per cent body weight) dehydration, such as fatigue, increased risk of heat illness and decreased performance if not taken care of. We should drink fluids at regular intervals while exercising. In

---

[16]"Hickline, Tianna, Yoga Eases Moderate to Severe Chronic Low Back Pain', *National Institutes of Health (NIH)*, 2017, http://tinyurl.com/mrh2hsy7. Accessed on 3 January 2024.

general, for exercises that take less than 60 minutes, water is appropriate. When exercising for more than 60 minutes, sports drinks provide energy and electrolytes (sodium and potassium), which can prevent muscle cramps.

Nutrition and hydration are also important post-exercise. The electrolytes (sodium and potassium) that are lost in sweat and the carbohydrates utilized need to be replenished. Post-exercise protein helps to repair damaged muscle tissue and to stimulate the growth of muscle mass. Nutritional recovery should begin within 15–60 minutes following exercise. Replace fluid and potassium losses by consuming fruits and vegetables. Combine carbohydrate and protein sources.

Dietary Supplements

Once we start an exercise regime, one of the most common questions that crops up is about supplements. Should we take supplements? Which supplements are safe, effective and legal?

A well-balanced diet with whole foods can safely give complete nutrition and energy for optimal performance. If extra nutrition is required, try supplementing it with whole foods rather than artificial supplements. A good dietitian can help devise a nutrition plan that can cater to your individual needs. Always choose food over supplements to improve your performance.

It is important to know and adhere to the nutritional/dietary supplement regulations. People taking dietary supplements should understand that bad manufacturing processes and the risk of contamination increase the chance of unknowingly consuming banned supplements that can be hazardous to health. While the regulations for manufacturing dietary supplements is stringent, they are not always enforceable. Therefore, there can be no guarantee of a product's purity, safety or effectiveness. It is better to consult a specialist before taking any supplements.

Furthermore, supplements are very expensive, and it is perhaps best that we get our nutrition from a balanced diet.

Table 1: Common dietary supplements, their risks and food equivalents[17]

Supplements	Risks	Food Equivalents
Multivitamins and minerals	Potential toxicity if taken in amounts that are greater than recommended	Meats, poultry, fish, whole grains, vegetables, fruits, beans and peas, nuts, low-fat dairy
Caffeine	Potential anxiety, irritability, insomnia, headaches, gastrointestinal (GI) distress	Coffee, tea, chocolate
Creatine	GI distress, cramps, potential contamination	Meat, poultry, fish
Protein and added amino acids	Potential contamination	Beef, pork, chicken, fish, turkey, beans, lentils, tofu, tempeh, nuts, eggs, low-fat dairy
Omega-3 fatty acids	Potential contamination	Fatty fish (salmon), flaxseed oil, walnuts, canola oil

---

[17]'Understanding Dietary Supplements', *Sports, Cardiovascular, and Wellness Nutrition Registered Dieticians (SCAN RDs)*, 2013.

If you are keen to take supplements, then do your homework. Be aware of three significant factors about nutrition supplementation: safety, compliance and regulations and efficacy.

1. **Safety:** The food and drug administration authorities of countries do NOT regulate the supplement industry. This means there is NO guarantee that the supplement you are taking is pure and not tainted with something that should not be in the product. Keep in mind that 'natural' does not equal 'safe'.
2. **Compliance**: Many supplements are available at stores, like caffeine tablets, ephedrine and norandrostenediol, to name a few. Just because you can buy a product at the store does not mean its use is acceptable or recommended. Always do your research. Ask questions whether the product's listed side effects outweigh its perceived benefits and whether it is worth risking your health.
3. **Efficacy:** Despite all of the rules and regulations, there are still many supplements available that can benefit an athlete. It has been proven that electrolyte replacement drinks can aid with hydration and performance. Nutrition shakes after weight training sessions can aid in muscle recovery and replenish muscle glycogen (the storage form of energy in the muscles). Some female athletes benefit greatly from a daily iron supplement, as they can be at increased risk of anaemia. However, the efficacy of many others is still under question and thorough research must be undertaken to prevent consumption of ineffectual, even potentially harmful substances.

While these options may prove effective, no single food, drink, supplement, meal or snack can enhance performance entirely on its own. Keep in mind that an optimal training diet meets a person's caloric needs with an appropriate protein, fat and carbohydrate balance. A balanced and varied eating plan will also deliver appropriate amounts of vitamins and minerals. Everything we eat works together to meet our energy demands.

In conclusion, exercise is needed for a better long-term quality of life, and there is a level of exercise that is suitable for everyone. It is essential to be careful and start exercising under supervision. Proper guidance can give better results with comparatively lesser effort.

KEY POINTS

1. Physical activity and physical fitness are different things.
2. It is important to go 'low and slow' when starting to exercise, that is, start with low intensity and increase exercise intensity gradually.
3. Aim for some form of exercise daily.
4. Supplements can help but are not essential for fitness. A balanced diet is sufficient in most cases.
5. People engaged in vigorous sports or high-intensity workouts may need supplements, but care needs to be taken before consuming them.
6. Encourage your friends to exercise regularly.
7. Exercise not only improves physical health but also does wonders for the mental health of the person.
8. Sleep remains an essential constituent of recovery. Don't ignore it.

8

SEX, SEXUALITY AND SEXUAL ORIENTATION

> *'Sex education is not only about having sex, but it is also important to look at the health and reproductive system, and protect the body from infections.'*
>
> —SID NAING

Let's do a flashback to Class 8 when the chapter on reproductive health was being taught in Biology class. The students would have butterflies in the stomach with excitement and would also be conscious of not smiling, giggling and not making eye contact with the teacher. The teacher would also be hypervigilant and would be on the lookout for students sniggering in class.

But does it have to be that way? We, as a society, need to be more open and talk about such things with ease. And the sooner, the better.

Adolescence is a crucial time between childhood and adulthood. It is a transitional stage encompassing tremendous physical, emotional, sexual and mental development.

Adolescents often see sex as a rite of passage for transitioning into adulthood. But adolescent sexuality and its perception has seen many changes over the last few decades, with adolescents now reaching physical and sexual maturity earlier.[18] Rapid technological changes have posed many newer challenges in dealing with adolescent sexual behaviour and its risks, but it also has its benefits.

Puberty heralds a set of physical and hormonal changes linked with the onset of sexual thoughts and experimentation. Adolescents' decision-making about matters of sexual and reproductive health depends on their knowledge, which is based on the society they live in, their family environment, role models, friends, siblings and what they have seen in popular culture. The information they have, and more importantly do not have, can affect their lives in the long run; therefore, a good understanding of sexual issues and sexual knowledge is essential to ensure that adolescents are well-informed and aware about everything related to sex and sexuality.

Pubertal Changes

With the onset of puberty, specific physical changes occur in both boys and girls. In boys, there is body hair growth (axillary, pubic, moustache and beard), the voice breaks and becomes deeper and the genitals grow in size. In girls, there is the enlargement of breasts, body hair growth (axillary and pubic) and the beginning of menstruation. Adolescents can

---

[18]Ohlsson, Claes, et al., 'Secular Trends in Pubertal Growth Acceleration in Swedish Boys Born from 1947 to 1996', *JAMA Pediatrics*, Vol. 173, No. 9, 2019, pp. 860, http://tinyurl.com/mr3y3aw8. Accessed on 3 January 2024.

become increasingly conscious of their body image. These changes are a part of growing up and adequate guidance from parents, older siblings or any trusted adult can help you make better sense of them.

Masturbation

Masturbation is the act of genital stimulation for sexual pleasure, which may or may not lead to orgasm. Masturbation is quite common among males and females of all ages and plays a vital role in healthy sexual development.

There are many myths about masturbation that may cause feelings of guilt and shame. None of the myths or claims on masturbation are backed by scientific evidence. Studies have shown several benefits of masturbation, which include reduced stress, enhanced sleep quality, the release of sexual tension, elevation of mood and improved concentration.

There is no right or wrong in terms of the frequency of masturbation, but do seek help if masturbation starts interfering with your daily life, studies or relationship with your family or friends.

Sex, Sexual Identity and Sexual Orientation

Sexual attraction begins in late childhood or early adolescence and can lead to romantic and/or sexual relationships. It is also not uncommon for children and adolescents to experience same-sex attractions. Both heterosexual and homosexual experimentations are common among adolescents.

Nikhil is a 32-year-old successful chartered accountant and is gay. He has never been able to tell anyone in his family. He feels that they would not understand. His family started pressurising him to get married, and after a few years, he relented and agreed to get married. He and his wife split up after three months of marriage.

The above scenario is very common. Homonegativity is a deeply entrenched problem in our society, so much so that homosexual individuals are often brought to hospitals to 'treat' them. It is essential to understand that this is not an illness. Acceptance and understanding of different sexual identities remains a challenge.

The terms 'sex', 'sexual and gender identity' and 'sexual orientation' can be quite tricky to understand and differentiate. Sex stands for biological sex assigned at birth; it could be male, female or intersex. Sexual or gender identity refers to the gender a person feels connected to. So, a biological man may identify as a woman, and a biological woman may feel that they are actually a man. This identity is referred to as being transgender. And sexual orientation is about who a person is emotionally, romantically and/or sexually attracted to. Here are a few types of sexual orientations that people around the world have, and what they mean:

1. **Heterosexual:** Being attracted towards the opposite sex.
2. **Homosexual:** Being attracted towards people of the same sex. The word 'gay' describes a man who is attracted to men, and 'lesbian' refers to a woman who is attracted to women.
3. **Bisexual:** Being attracted towards people of both the individual's own sex and of the opposite sex.
4. **Asexual:** People having no interest in sexual relationships.

5. **Pansexual:** People who have sexual attraction towards all gender types.

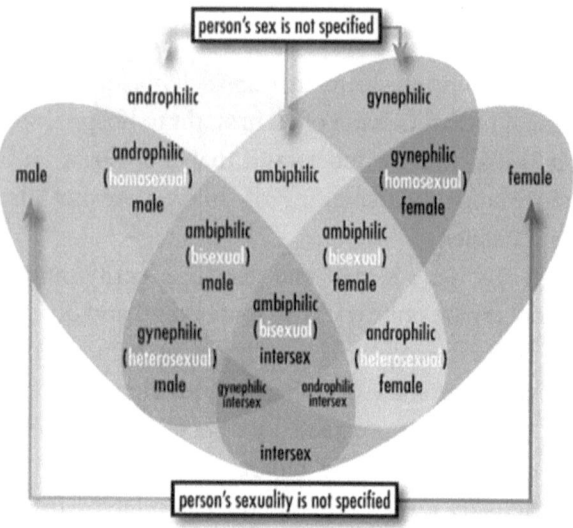

Figure 15: A Venn diagram of a few types of sexualities[19]

'Philia' means fondness, 'andro' stands for male and 'gyne' refers to female. As you can see from the above diagram, sex, sexuality and sexual orientation can be quite confusing to understand. Despite that, we should always treat people with dignity and a non-judgemental attitude as you would yourself like to be treated.

Unfortunately, discrimination based on sexual identity and orientation remains quite rife in society. It is, however, much better than before, but a lot still needs to be done. Ignorance

---

[19]James, Andrea, 'Sex-Sexuality-Venn', http://tinyurl.com/jjdyzz5j, licensed under CC BY-SA 3.0 DEED.

remains the most significant barrier, and the fear of being judged, being outed or being the victim of a hate crime remains an obstacle in people coming out. Coming out of the closet, often shortened to 'coming out', is a metaphor used to describe LGBTQIA+ people's self-disclosure of their sexual orientation, romantic orientation or gender identity. The further fear of reduced career prospects also increases their emotional and financial insecurity.

Needless to say, homonegativity is an ethical crime, even if it's not a legal one yet.

Sexually Transmitted Diseases (STDs)

Sexually active adolescents are at a higher risk of acquiring STDs due to psychological, behavioural, physiological and environmental factors. As teens begin to experiment, their chances of engaging in risky sexual behaviour increase.

The most common STDs are chlamydia, human papilloma virus (HPV), syphilis, gonorrhoea, trichomonas and HIV infections.

Prevention, easy diagnosis and treatment are available for most STDs. Both partners should get tested for STDs before engaging in sex, and ensure that they use a condom from start to finish every time they have sex. It is vital to talk to your partner about how you both would prevent STDs and—in case of a heterosexual relationship—pregnancy, before initiating a sexual relationship. They should also discuss what they are comfortable with and set boundaries before they start. You always have a right to say no, and your partner should respect that.

Make sure you have the adequate knowledge and healthcare support that you need. Consider asking a doctor or nurse about STD testing and vaccines available against HPV and hepatitis B. A lot of STDs are asymptomatic, and you may not notice any symptoms. Getting medical tests done is the only way to know whether you or your partner have any STDs. Some places offer teen-friendly, confidential and free STD tests. STDs like chlamydia and gonorrhoea can easily be treated with antibiotics. Other STDs, like herpes, can't be cured, but you can take medication to help with the symptoms.

Unplanned Pregnancy

Unplanned and early pregnancies are a significant health and social concern for most countries. About 21 million girls aged 15–19 years in developing countries become pregnant each year, and around 12 million of them give birth. According to a World Health Organization report from 2023, at least 777,000 births occur each year to girls younger than 15 years in developing countries.

Avoiding pregnancies may be difficult for adolescents due to knowledge gaps, poor communication and misconceptions on where to obtain contraceptives and how to use them. Adolescents face barriers when accessing contraception due to social stigma, strict laws and policies regarding the availability of contraceptives based on their age, marital status, health worker's bias and an adolescent's own inability to access contraceptives because of knowledge gap, lack of availability and financial constraints.

When a girl becomes pregnant, her life, unfortunately, can change drastically. She may be unable to continue her education and her career prospects reduce drastically. She may suffer from social exclusion and become vulnerable to poverty, and her physical and mental health suffers. Additionally, adolescent pregnancies have a higher chance of complications, both during term and delivery. Moreover, children born to ill-equipped parents who aren't mentally, emotionally and economically prepared may be subject to less-than-suitable home environments, which can result in abuse and bullying.

Personal misconceptions and biases hamper the efforts to address such issues. Most people find fault with the girl and aim only to change their behaviours rather than addressing the underlying early pregnancy drivers. This results in social exclusions, gender inequality, poverty, emotional abuse, childhood sexual abuse and negative attitude towards girls and women. Most efforts also neglect to account for the role of boys and men.

Adolescence is a time for laying the foundation for the future. It is normal, and even encouraged, that teenagers explore their sexuality. Seek and obtain knowledge about contraception and safe sexual practices from your doctor or reliable sources from the Internet. Do not ignore missed periods or any change in your physical health. In case of an unplanned pregnancy, it's only wise to confide in your parents and seek medical help.

Child Sexual Abuse

Child sexual abuse refers to an activity in which a person engages in sexual activity with a minor to gain sexual pleasure, stimulation or sexual gratification. Abusers are mostly (but not exclusively) males. They usually belong to the child's closest environment and are people they love and trust. Children should be taught to be wary of inappropriate touching and body language. A 'good touch' makes people feel warm, connected and safe. 'Bad touch' refers to any form of contact that is unasked for and that makes us feel uncomfortable.

Girls are three times more likely to be abused than boys. Sexual abuse can have devastating consequences on the life of the child who suffers abuse and can lead to a severe impact on the child's emotions and behaviours, ultimately hampering their growth and development. It has been linked to educational difficulties, poor psychological functioning, interpersonal relationship, risk-taking and aggressive behaviour, and alcohol and drug dependence.

It is essential to be aware of your surroundings and avoid vulnerable situations. It is okay to say 'no' to any unwanted or unwelcome touch, gesture or behaviour, even when it comes from your parents or trusted elders. It does not mean that you are disrespecting them; only that you are setting healthy boundaries. Report any verbal, sexual, physical or emotional abuse to your parents, teachers or to authorities who can help you.

Pornography

The Internet affords adolescents free and easy access to anonymous sexual misinformation, and smartphones give them ongoing access to social networking, instant messaging and other media. This easy availability may result in more exposure to sexual content than traditional media. Adolescents now get much of their information about and exposure to sexual content on the Internet, which is quite an unregulated space. The evolving nature of technologically-mediated pornographic content (e.g., real-time and interactional) provides novelty and variety at unprecedented speeds. Thus, the rise of the Internet has given new urgency to the issue of pornography.

Children and adolescents are the most vulnerable audiences to sexually explicit material. Internet pornography may threaten many facets of adolescent development and well-being. Exposure to bad pornography may lead to personal insecurities about their bodies, appearance or sexual performance. It may reduce attachment, leading to relationship dysfunction and, later, social isolation. Viewing unconventional pornography promotes sexual aggression, risky sexual practices and the objectification of women. Additionally, the risk of cyber-bullying, sexual victimization or harassment from others is real and all-pervasive.

Recent research indicates that adolescents are increasingly struggling with compulsive Internet use (CIU) and compulsive behaviours related to Internet pornography and cybersex.[20]

It is important to realize that most Internet pornography does not reflect real-life situations. It depicts sex as driven solely by pleasure-seeking and not associated with love, affection or a committed relationship. Excess consumption of pornography may lead to unusual expectations from self or partner. Pornography can become addictive and interfere with studies, social life, and relationships with parents, siblings and friends. One must confide in parents or close friends or relatives who can give effective guidance and offer proper professional help and counselling.

However, pornography can have some advantages too. It can be considered an uncomplicated process of expressing

---

[20] Balhara, Yatan Pal Singh, et al., 'Problematic Internet Use and Its Correlates among Students from Three Medical Schools across Three Countries', *Academic Psychiatry*, Vol. 39, No. 6, pp. 634–638, 2015, http://tinyurl.com/mr43kdw9. Accessed 3 January 2024.

sexual desires and it can shelter teenagers from complicated sexual hassles early in their life. Studies have also shown that as the availability of pornography has increased, there has been no increase in sex crimes.[21] The accessibility of pornography may narrow the gap for access to formal sex education classes. Nevertheless, it has to be exposure to the right type of pornography and at an appropriate age that has a positive impact and not a negative one.

In summary, talking about sex and sexual education remains an uncomfortable topic in families and schools. Parents of adolescents need to understand and accept that their children are maturing, and if they have a good knowledge base about sex, they can keep themselves safe. These discussions should start sooner rather than later.

KEY TIPS FOR PARENTS

1. Children need acceptance, comfort and guidance. Counsel them about the changes in their bodies, answer their queries patiently and help them cope with these changes in a healthy manner. Educate them about maintaining hygiene and taking care of their needs without making them feel guilty or embarrassed about it. Also, give them more privacy.
2. Communication and trust are the keys to improving relationships with the child and increasing your awareness about the culture and society that your child is growing up in.
3. The child's trust in their parent's ability to listen and understand can make a world of difference. Accept and support them but also be vigilant. Your children need you during these turbulent times more than they are ready to accept.

---

[21]Diamond, Milton, 'Pornography, Public Acceptance and Sex Related Crime: A Review', *International Journal of Law and Psychiatry*, Vol. 32, No. 5, pp. 304–14, 2009, http://tinyurl.com/w3hjj4m5. Accessed on 3 January 2024.

4. It's important to establish an open channel of communication so that you can guide your child towards safe sexual practices, and they can seek your help without inhibition.
5. It is also important that parents develop an Internet safety plan to reduce the likelihood of exposure to sexual material for young children on the home computer and mobile devices. For young children, limit alone and unsupervised Internet use. Encourage Internet use in only public areas of the home. At the same time, parents must be cautious because being too restrictive with older children and adolescents may lead them to be less open and honest regarding online behaviour.
6. Masturbation is a safe sexual activity. Do not chastise your child for the same. Rather, use it as an opportunity to discuss sexual health further.
7. Early on in their childhood, teach them the importance of good and bad touch. Never ignore hints, complaints or the tell-tale signs of abuse. Support them, as they are not the ones at fault. Muster the courage to take corrective action, even if it's against a friend/relative.
8. Every child grows up differently and will reach both physical and emotional maturity at different times. Do consult a doctor if there is an unusual delay in the onset of pubertal changes. A 'well-being' appointment with a urologist, gynaecologist or a family physician privately in the early years may allow the adolescent to feel able to ask questions that they may have. Timely action can protect them from long-term adverse consequences.
9. Unfortunately, sometimes things can go wrong, whether it is problematic masturbation, excessive exposure to pornography or STDs. Do consider a session with a psychologist or psychiatrist to provide support to the young person and yourself.
10. Strive for a relationship with your teen that is affectionate, firm, rich in communication and one that emphasizes mutual trust and respect.

9

WOMEN'S HEALTH AND CONTRACEPTION

'Safe sex is an act of self-love.'

—MIYA YAMANOUCHI

The adolescent years lay the foundation for a young person's understanding and value systems about sex and sexuality. While the two words are often used interchangeably, they imply two different and fundamental aspects of human character.

At the outset, an adolescent must thoroughly understand the act of sex. In modern times, a rather rudimentary sex education about the physiology of reproduction is provided to average pre-adolescent children in schools. Education about what to expect in terms of changing physical appearances with the development of secondary sexual characters is also conveyed. Girls usually undergo physical changes even before they are teenagers. There is breast development, change in the body's shape, appearance of axillary and pubic hair, and menstrual cycles.

As the body evolves to carry out the function of procreation, the mind also adapts to deal with the changes. Some young girls may wish they did not have visible growth changes. A girl who starts her menstrual cycle needs emotional support and training on how to manage her periods and what she should expect during her cycle. Questions, misconceptions and fears plague the minds of most adolescents, and it becomes the duty of those around them to ensure that every question and fear they have is adequately and correctly addressed.

Nikita, an 18-year-old, has recently moved to a foreign country for further studies. Being very sociable, she finds it easy to make friends. She has been in a relationship for the last three months. Her boyfriend feels that they should be progressive, and as they like each other, they should start a sexual relationship. She doesn't know what to do or who to speak to. Coming from a conservative family, she feels that they would be highly opposed to this.

There may be internal and external conflicts that can aggravate a situation like this. An open and positive parent–child relationship can go a long way in providing the correct balance between the yes-es and no-es during this period. Right from self-image, clothing, attitude, self-expression, to the company of the correct people, educational institutions and places visited for other areas of interest, all have a significant role in making the human character and belief in what is right and wrong.

Even though there is an excess of information available, it is not uncommon that educated youngsters could have wrongly understood the physiology of reproduction. The correct understanding of the menstrual and reproductive cycle is very important. The adolescent should correctly understand the time of ovulation, its normal range of variation and the window of possibility of getting pregnant. Along with this, she must be advised about the physiology of conception, contraception and prevention of sexually transmitted diseases.

Even highly educated couples can misunderstand the safe period and not use condoms during the ovulation window. Traditional education does not make one wiser on this subject. The use of condoms for pregnancy prevention and STDs in every act of sex can never be overemphasized.

To reiterate a very valid ideology of handholding, it cannot be emphasized enough how crucial it is to hold hands with adolescents when it comes to sex and sexuality. Parental handholding and providing a safe space to share even embarrassing situations is the best way forward. If not the parents, then an elder sibling, family member or friend who is both more experienced than and concerned for the adolescent's welfare can step in and have the conversation with the adolescent that needs to be had.

Well-being meetings with gynaecologists can help young girls get an opportunity to gain professional advice about the prevention of STDs and unwanted pregnancies. Many adolescent girls suffer from polycystic ovaries and irregular cycles. For them, it is even more important to consult their doctor regularly.

Adolescent boys mature physically a bit later than girls. Secondary sexual characters start developing around 12 and 13 years of age. The facial and body hair slowly increases and becomes coarser. The torso also changes with a broader chest and shoulders. The genital organs gain pigmentation and increase in size.

Along with changes in physical attributes, teenage boys undergo a lot of emotional changes. Like girls, they also experience internal conflict about becoming an adult versus staying the way they are. Having a set of well-defined boundaries helps inculcate good self-discipline at this very tender age. In case rules are broken, empathy and patience are needed to deal with the situation. If a responsible adult understands why a particular behaviour was displayed and appropriate corrective action is taken, it will help positively shape personality.

Suppose a father catches his son getting physical with a girl in the house. Instead of rage, an empathetic, open approach would help both the parent and teenager. There are many life lessons that could be taught here, such as always treating your partner with the utmost respect, and that, in case the relationship breaks up and the partner moves on, there should be no humiliation or guilt for either party.

Young boys start experiencing erections and night emissions. There is much curiosity and need to understand one's own body and the physiology of erections and ejaculation. Thorough education about masturbation can help both girls and boys to not feel ashamed or awkward about masturbation.

Youngsters are not naive. They are aware that apart from normal penovaginal intercourse, there can be oral or anal intercourse. They may want to experiment when it comes to sexual activity. The importance of open and honest communication, the endeavour to equip them both mentally and emotionally, and taking a sensitive approach cannot be overemphasized.

During the phase of attaining sexual maturity, a teenager can question and experiment with their sexual identity. In certain circumstances, a teenager may have homosexual or bisexual preferences. In such a situation, professional help is almost always crucial to maintain a positive relationship between teenagers and their families. I would like to give the example of a family from a low socioeconomic background that brought their 18-year-old child to a clinic for gender-affirming surgery. The entire family was very concerned and supportive of them during the whole period of hospitalization, which helped the young person immensely in dealing with the emotional and physical changes.

Contraception

Having an understanding of contraception in adolescence is of utmost importance. It is also essential to understand all the available options as different options may be more suitable at different stages of life. An unwanted pregnancy can cause a lot of emotional trauma, and the need and process of undergoing a medical or surgical abortion can be very distressing.

Various methods to prevent unwanted pregnancy could be:

- Calendar method (unsafe days are from day 8 till day 18 for a girl with a 28-day menstrual cycle)
- Withdrawal method (ejaculation outside the vagina)
- Barrier method (condoms)
- Vaginal anti spermicidal pessary
- Oral contraceptive pills
- Intrauterine hormone devices

Oral hormonal options can be of two types:

1. Low dose 21-day oestrogen-progesterone combination pill (OC pills) to be taken every cycle.
2. A single tablet of high dose progesterone (I-Pill/Pill 72) to be consumed within 72 hours of unprotected sex.

No method can be called 100 per cent safe, and usually, a combination of methods should be used. Failure rates are the lowest with oral 21-day pills and with intrauterine progesterone releasing devices. A condom should be used each time to prevent not just pregnancy but also sexually transmitted diseases.

Other methods like calendar, withdrawal and emergency pill have higher failure rates and should only be used in case of emergencies such as the rupture of condoms, or in combination with another method (e.g., condoms with withdrawal method).

In case of frequent sex and long-term requirement of protection against unwanted pregnancy, 21-day OC pills and an intrauterine progesterone releasing device would be the most effective.

KEY POINTS

1. Correct sex education at school is a must just before the onset of puberty.
2. Adolescence is the time when one first starts understanding what sex is and starts developing their sexuality. They have sexual attractions and try to understand their sexual identity.
3. A knowledgeable and compassionate adult/parent can do wonders for a teenager in the 'teething stage' of sex and sexuality.
4. In unpleasant situations around sex, empathy with firmness will help build a positive attitude.
5. Masturbation, pornography and altered sexual behaviours are all subjects that need to be handled with the utmost care.
6. Prevention of unwanted pregnancy and STDs in each act of sex can never be overemphasized.
7. Seek professional help early if situations feel out of control.

Part 3
CAREERS AND FINANCE

'Begin somewhere; you cannot build a reputation on what you intend to do.'

—LIZ SMITH

10

THE DREADED EXAMS

'Trust yourself; you know more than you think you do.'

—DR BENJAMIN SPOCK

Each of us has had to give examinations, and most believe that they are a nuisance. We have all heard and read stories about students' struggles with exams. Sometimes people go to extreme lengths to study better or respond badly when they fail.

Take a moment to think about your usual exam strategy and what exams and their results mean to you. Are you a planner who would make a study plan? Or are you a person who would want to study as much as possible and squeeze every last ounce of energy or motivation out of yourself? Or are you a carefree person who doesn't mind winging it?

Examinations are an integral part of the education system and cause much stress for most students. The anxiety and stress around the exams kick in the extra adrenaline, which helps with focus and concentration, and usually allows the students to put in the extra effort into preparing for their exams. Still, the same stress can make some students buckle under the pressure.

Educationists have been debating for many decades about a better method of judging students' competence. Most people agree that a well-rounded assessment of a student should include their performance over the whole year rather than just an end-of-year exam. These assessments should include a variety of evaluations like a practical approach, the critical appraisal of topics, drama, debates and projects. Every system has its limitations, and thus, no clear and acceptable answer has yet been found or agreed upon. Therefore, examinations (in whichever form) are here to stay despite their limitations.

People who support the current examination system feel that exams help build confidence while making a child aware of hard work, patience and goal setting.

Exams can help with the following:

1. **Maintain focus**: If there are no exams, then the students may not focus on studying.
2. **Inculcate dedication and discipline**: It trains people to work hard towards a goal with commitment.
3. **Manage time:** It teaches students about the importance of time management—both while preparing for and giving an exam. This lays the foundation of better time management.
4. **Work under pressure:** Exams are pressure situations, and having the confidence of having previously worked well under pressure can help students manage life situations better. It is a given that pressures will, inevitably, come into their life.
5. **Improve learning and brain power**: When we study, new neural circuits are made, which make our brain

stronger. The concept is no different than when we lift weights and the arm muscles become stronger.
6. **Self-assessment and reflection:** Examinations give the student an idea about what they are good at and help them decide future careers.

Educationists use the same set of arguments to argue against the exam system.

1. They can cause **undue stress and increase competition** between students at an early stage of life.
2. The exam system can **scar people for life** and can cause low self-confidence and low self-esteem if they are not great at studies.
3. It can push students to **cram and memorize** books rather than encouraging them to make an effort to understand them.
4. Students who haven't done well are **judged by others,** and all the other good skills they may possess are neglected.
5. **The one-size-fits-all examination policy** is not suitable for all students because each student has different strengths and weaknesses.
6. If the stress in a student is not treated, it **can lead to mental disorders**, including anxiety, depression and suicidality.

Whichever side of this debate one stands on, the reality is that, at the present time, one has to go through exams to progress in life and exams have to be negotiated as best as possible.

Preparing for Exams

Each set of examinations should be looked at as an independent project, and project management and problem-solving skills should be used to negotiate them. We have already discussed the SMART technique of managing exam prep in the chapter on managing failures.

Generally, exam stress can be managed, and with proper planning and discipline, students can achieve their potential.

Some useful tips to tackle exams:

1. **Know your syllabus**: Divide your syllabus into 'Essentials' and 'Desirables'. Essentials are a part of your syllabus that holds the most value. Ensure that you know those before moving to the 'Desirables' part of the syllabus. Desirables include topics that are less likely to be asked in exams.
2. **Keep your workspace clean and less busy**: A cluttered work space increases distractions and reduces the efficiency of your efforts.
3. **Know your limitations**: In general, a good concentration period is about 45–60 minutes. Take a 5–10-minute break after studying for about 45–60 minutes.
4. **Get good sleep**: Sleep is the most powerful natural efficiency enhancer. A well-rested mind is able to absorb and retain more.
5. **Eat healthy:** A good mix of fruits and vegetables ensures that an optimum portion of vitamins and minerals, which help energy and concentration, reach the body.
6. **Make a study group:** Studying with similar or mixed-ability students can help you understand your material

better. Studying with people of superior ability will make you feel less confident and, similarly, doing so with people of lower aptitude can give you false confidence.
7. **Don't over revise**: There will always be areas that you feel you haven't studied for or know well enough. You always know more than what you think you know.
8. **Avoid the excess intake of caffeine and sugary foods**: These products can increase anxiety, irritability and disturb one's sleep.
9. **Regular exercise:** Exercising/playing sports and stretching regularly help keep the mind fresh and maintain a positive attitude towards life.
10. **Be flexible**: Make a schedule but don't be too hard on yourself if you can't achieve your target on a particular day. Focus on making incremental progress and not perfection.
11. **Rewarding yourself for achieving targets**: This can include watching an episode of your favourite series or going out for a meal.
12. **Reducing mobile phone use**: Turn off all notifications on your phone and try to check social media only 1–2 times per day.
13. **Resting in-between exams**: Once an exam is over, there is no point thinking about it. It is important to rest before preparing for the next one.
14. **Seek help:** If you are struggling, then speak to your parents, teachers or friends and ask for help.

It is also important to realize that, sometimes, increasing efforts will not result in an improvement in one's scores. As mentioned earlier, this relationship is linear until a certain point (let's say until 100 per cent). After that, a lot of effort may be needed to make smaller increments. If we try too hard, then output may actually come down.

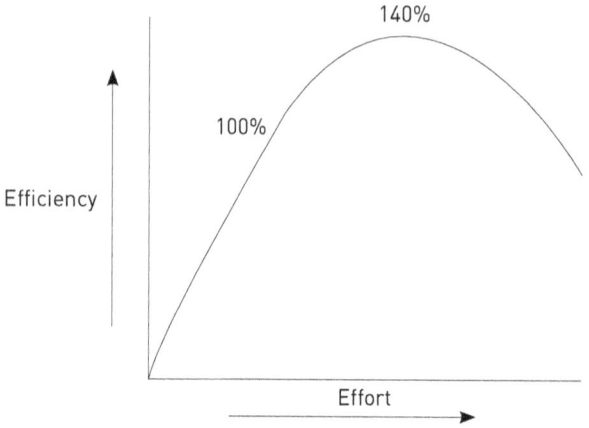

Figure 16: The relationship between efficiency and effort

Nandini, a student of Class 10, thinks that Mathematics is a dreadful subject. Though she does well in other subjects, her performance in Mathematics is average. This leaves her teachers and parents in wonder as she does quite well in class assignments and discussions. She complains that she loses her bearings when she sees the question paper. Her heart starts pounding and she starts sweating as soon as she gets the question paper. All her acquired knowledge in the subject fades away during the examination.

However, after proper counselling by her parents, teachers and school counsellors, she has been able to control her fear and improve her scores in the subject.

A child's school examination is usually a stressful time for parents too. Parents need to look after themselves so that their stress does not get transferred to their children. They should ensure that they take time out for themselves to manage their own stress. They should also spend time with their child doing things outside of studying to reduce their pressure as well.

The Day of the Exam

On the day of your exam, try to follow your usual morning routine and eat a healthy breakfast. Hopefully, you would have slept well the night before and you wake up feeling rested and alert. Keep yourself hydrated and avoid tea and coffee. Take a few deep breaths, trust your instincts and you should be good to go. Remember: the marker for success is not the marks you score but the effort that you have put into doing your best.

Some anxiety during the exam is good as it releases adrenaline which helps us concentrate better. But if you feel tense during the exam, then attempt the easier questions to build up confidence. Then, stretch a little in your seat, take deep breaths and drink a little water. After this little break, try the tougher questions once again.

After the Exam

Take some time off before preparing for the next exam. Regardless of whether the day's exam has gone well, the next one is a different project and has to be negotiated differently. Reward and treat yourself for your previous effort and start again. The goal is to do your best and nothing else.

Once your whole set of exams are done, there is nothing more for you to do other than await the results. Make the best use of the downtime by engaging in meaningful and productive activities. Play sports, exercise and meet friends. If the result is as expected, then we move on to the next challenge in life. If, however, it is not what was expected, we accept it as a learning experience and improve ourselves for the next examination.

In summary, exams are events that are to be negotiated as best as possible. Some anxiety is helpful, but stressing yourself out and worrying about the result can hamper your abilities.

Remember, you are much more than just an exam result.

KEY POINTS

How can parents support their children during exams?

1. **Watch for signs of stress in your child:** Pessimistic or negative thinking, having headaches, irritability, loss of appetite and poor sleep are all signs of stress.
2. **Encourage your child to talk:** Talking about their difficulties and apprehensions can go a long way in reducing their stress.
3. **Manage your child's and your own expectations:** While it is important to maintain a positive mindset, striking a balance between optimism and realism is also important.
4. **Make sure they eat well:** A hungry body doesn't study well. Make sure they keep themselves hydrated, too.
5. **Give them rewards:** Rewards and treats in between, however small, can help maintain the motivation to study.
6. **Make sure they sleep well:** As mentioned above, sleep is the most powerful ability enhancer we have. So, encourage them to get enough sleep.

7. **'All work and no play, makes Jack a dull boy':** Encourage exercise, hobbies and meeting friends to keep their mind fresh and active.
8. **Help them study:** Offer to do some of their chores and help them avoid non-essential work, so that they can focus more on studies.
9. **Be flexible and available:** Make sure that you are there when they need you.
10. **Seek professional help:** If you feel your child is stressed or struggling, a single session with a psychologist, counsellor or a psychiatrist can go a long way.

11

CAREER CHOICES AND HOW TO MAKE THEM

'Choose a job you love, and you will never have to work a day in your life.'

—CONFUCIUS

Close your eyes for thirty seconds and imagine yourself doing exactly what you want to do.

How amazing would it feel if you were able to work in a field you love?

Take a moment to think about:

- what career you want to pursue.
- how you came to that decision.

Shakespeare wrote, 'Some are born great, some achieve greatness, and some have greatness thrust upon them.' I think this is true for careers, too. Some people know what they want to do in life, some find a direction for themselves with time while others have careers given to them.

Sometimes, people change professions as they go through life. Brad Pitt and Akshay Kumar used to work as a driver and a chef, respectively. The author Stephen King was a janitor, and Gulzar used to work in a garage. There are countless examples of people who have changed their profession successfully later in life. It is okay to acknowledge that it is not an easy decision to make and is not completely set in stone.

We all have to make career choices; sometimes, it comes naturally to us and sometimes, it is born out of necessity and one's circumstances. An integral part of choosing a career is decision-making. Decision-making is a process that involves primarily five points that any teenager would need to consider, especially when it comes to choosing a career:

1. **Interest**: What you always thought you would want to do.
2. **Acumen/Talent**: What you are really good at.
3. **Passion:** what makes you give it your all?
4. **Family and Finances**: Your environment and your financial capability.
5. **Experience**: What you have grown up seeing around you or grown up doing.

Let us take a peek into some real-life cases that can help you relate to and understand what each one of the factors implies, especially when we are growing up! They may also help us make good decisions.

Let's understand what each one of them entails.

Interests

An interest is something you want to do, invest your time in and would want to be. For example, you could be interested in becoming a football player or an actor or an army officer. It is something that catches your fancy when you are young and stays with you as you grow up, or it could be something that someone you look up to does. If your favourite uncle is an army officer, it might develop your interest in the army. Loving an actor might make you want to be like them.

Aaryan has grown up admiring his maternal uncle who is an army officer. Whenever the uncle came home, he would be full of stories of adventure and bravery. His picture library was dotted with amazing aircrafts, mountains and glaciers. Aaryan was in awe of his 'Mamu' and wished to follow in his footsteps.

As he grew up, however, he developed a keen interest in art. His paintings were auctioned by his school for a charitable cause when he was in Class 6. He continued to excel in art. In Class 7, one of his paintings was chosen to be the cover of a textbook. He went on to win several other accolades for himself and the school. Eventually, he joined a prestigious art school in India and continues to make his mark. He still remains in awe of his uncle and the armed forces.

It's worthwhile to note that we all possess a unique talent. It is merely a matter of discovering it. If you genuinely watch the actions and activities that you undertake, you will notice the natural tilt towards that particular activity by yourself. Once you find that unique thing/activity, you would also see how you start building everything automatically around it to accomplish the activity. An artist would reach for the canvas, brushes and paints, and a writer would start writing with the dream of writing a book someday. A foodie may aspire to become a culinary expert!

Another way to know whether your 'interest' is also your 'calling' is to dive deep into the field of your interest. Learn the ropes, understand the challenges and the rewards through proper research. You could join a club in school that promotes your interest or join online introductory classes to know more. There is a plethora of information available. Once you have narrowed down your interest, you could speak to your counsellor and use their help to explore further.

Did you as a child have a career in mind or did you look up to someone in your family or a celebrity? Are you still working towards that career, or do you feel that you are working towards something entirely different now? Interests can be dynamic, but they give us an idea about what may work for us in the future. Try and reflect on your interests.

Passion

Passion refers to a powerful desire for something. In pursuit of something that one is passionate about, you don't notice the passing of time. It makes you feel good about yourself, and you constantly want to better yourself at it and are willing to make sacrifices towards this goal.

Salil was absolutely engrossed in theatre and cricket in school. Academics took a back seat not because Salil lacked the inclination but because most of his time was spent pursuing the two things he loved the most. The school principal's office cabinet was stacked with Salil's trophies and awards that he had won. There was rarely a tournament or a performing arts event/ competition that he would not participate in and do well. He was a 'hero' to all his peers and juniors who adored him. The vibrancy this young man had as he transitioned into senior school was embedded in his personality. He immersed himself in the pursuit of his passion, even at the cost of his academic results.

Salil surprised everyone when he passed his Class 12 board exams with 80 per cent. He chose to study History for an undergraduate degree in a reputed college in Delhi. The college handpicked Salil not only because of his academic record but also because he was an excellent performer who scored well in his interview and group discussions. His confidence, his communication skills and application of knowledge stumped the jury just as he would stump the batsmen on the cricket field. Fortunately, his school provided him with the environment to grow his potential and excel. Salil's self-esteem and self-confidence multiplied as he progressed through school. The realization that academic marks weren't the only remit of a school reduced a lot of pressure that Salil put on himself. The myth that the best college isn't meant for an average boy who only scored 80 per cent was shattered when an elite college accepted Salil for being who he was!

That several careers can emerge through one's passions is what makes life interesting. There is an obvious investment of time and money in what you want to do, who you want to be and where you want to go. It is as much a part of your education as academics.

The important thing is making the decision to nurture your passion and exercise your talent.

Acumen

Acumen is one's natural ability to do something. Some kids are great at solving mathematics problems. Some are gifted sportsmen. Some are born with a melodious voice. Even though acumen is considered innate, it is great that you can learn and develop it through hard work and commitment. Your passion can guide you to develop the acumen for anything.

Many times, you may have a great interest and passion for an activity. However, your ability to perform it might not be all that brilliant. Sometimes, even though your passion guides you in one direction, your acumen points in another that was hitherto unknown.

16-year-old Sara sought career advice as she wanted to pursue a degree in Design Technology, Economics and Mathematics. After four months of studying Design Technology, she was confused about her choices and booked another appointment to discuss her options. Digging deeper, it was discovered that she had a tough time grasping the concepts and absorbing the technical material required for product design. After gathering more facts, it became evident that she genuinely enjoyed analysing and handling numbers. She could talk at length about economic issues and mathematical problem-solving.

What this example refers to is the fact that sometimes what appears attractive or fascinates us may not be where our natural acumen lies. Yes, you can equate it with aptitude, but there's a slight difference between the two. On one hand, it is critical to have an aptitude for a particular subject or discipline, but possessing the acumen for it keeps you motivated and enthusiastic. Acumen is the ability to respond, judge and process information quickly.

Sara got it! She realized that she was meant to pursue a career in Economics. She graduated in Econometrics last year and is happy with her job with an insurance company in Canada. She occasionally indulges in fashion design and helps her friends decide on dresses for important events.

One important finding that emerges in this case is that Sara learnt that there were options for her to explore further than what appeared initially. Applying this discretion, she was able to reach a potentially viable alternative career. When you engage yourself in the process of conscious decision-making, positive outcomes emerge invariably.

Family and Finances

We may know many people who have followed in their parents' footsteps. A doctor's kid goes on to become a doctor. Army officials generally have a history of serving in the army for multiple generations. A businessman's kid is more inclined to do an MBA and become an entrepreneur. The decision is mostly guided by the environment at home and the general expertise of the parents.

The best part about this is that you have accomplished role models at home. They are also individuals we unknowingly emulate as we transition to adulthood. A lot of our interests are acquired from them. The family steers your keenness towards a particular career. The environment at home incites your interest, and you gradually develop it. The environment also inspires you, and you begin doing things around what interests you.

Contrary to the former, there could be an environment that unfortunately does not inspire you, and you may face opposition in pursuing your interests. In that case, it depends on how you, as a teenager, convince your parents. One tried and tested approach is to display that talent or interest at school and outside. When parents see your passion for and commitment to it, they will encourage you to pursue it. Their doubts arise only when your actions do not match your words.

In both cases, the family's background and financial capability may impact your career choice. Therefore, it is critical to seek advice from an expert in the field and have both you and your parents meet with them to gain more insight. As kids, you are not usually privy to the financial situation at home. Therefore, it is a great idea to discuss it with your parents. It could be possible that the foreign university you were aiming for may not be feasible. In which case it may be a wise choice to look for something closer to home for undergraduate studies and work hard to earn a scholarship and pursue your dream abroad in a suitable master's program. Loans are an option that should be exercised with caution keeping in mind the capability to pay them back.

Anahita is a talented artist. On the strength of her portfolio and performance in Class 12, she managed to get a seat in the prestigious art school, Parsons, in New York. However, her father's business had recently suffered a jolt, and he could not pay the enormous fee that the college charges. Anahita understood the situation and applied to the best art schools in India. She got through one in Bangalore. She excelled at the school and won a competition for 100 per cent scholarship at a top art school in Paris for further studies.

Anahita's case tells us that it's okay to recalibrate your options based on your family situation.

There is definitely no reason for you to get upset, in case the dream choice didn't work out when you wanted it. Reaching your first-choice campus may be a choice that is delayed but not denied, especially if you persevere and set your targets correctly. You can wait for a better financial situation for your family to arise or create a possibility of funding your education by yourself.

Experience

As a student, you are exposed to various things which are not necessarily a part of your curriculum. Schools have several initiatives, such as Model United Nations (MUNs), adventure trips, social work, exchange programmes, learning trips within the country and abroad, etc. Additionally, your experience is further enriched by your vacations, the environment at home, neighbourhood and social media.

Who we are or become is a product of our experiences. An experienced individual is an enriched person. What is this enrichment? What does it mean for a teenager? It is simply the sum total of the wonderful or not-so-wonderful things that you do every day. Reading a book is an experience that expands your thinking and imagination. Listening to a good speech is inspiring. Watching a movie could be motivational or can invoke your creativity. Listening to a lecture could elevate your understanding of a particular concept. Attending a conference provides you with exposure to different ways of handling concerns. A hands-on experiment in a science laboratory builds your interest in the subject.

Mentorship programmes on topics of your interest can be a helpful resource. Mentorship can come from a senior professional in the area of work or a professor in the subject of your choice. There are several other ways of enriching your experiences. For instance, you could enrol yourself in a summer/winter program at a university. Universities offer a variety of them that can add value to your ongoing education and portfolio. With the growing need to give back to our community, one can take up social service. It gives you a sense of well-being when you work with people towards their welfare and upliftment. These activities can range from participating in teaching children, organizing donation camps and awareness campaigns for the underprivileged. Participating in such activities from a young age usually has a long-lasting positive impact on others and gives you a holistic perspective of the world. Being sensitive and caring towards others makes us better people. When we are better people, we make this world a better place to live in.

In conclusion, one common thing that has been seen in successful people is the open-minded approach to life. This is the best gift you can give yourself. Being an open-minded person will help you grow in a positive direction and strengthen your belief in yourself. You would be able to make decisions that are most suited to the situation while being cognizant of its impact on the future.

Maintaining focus on your tangible and long-term goals would undoubtedly pay off. Take pride in your journey, because you are the one making it. The major part of this journey is 'You'. The footprints that you leave behind will become your inspiration. Look back and see how everything becomes a milestone in your life.

KEY POINTS

1. It is important to acknowledge that making a career choice is one of the most difficult decisions one has to make in life.
2. For some, it comes easily but others need patience and perseverance. It is okay to take time to make this decision.
3. One should realize that the decision cannot be set in stone. It is okay to change your decision. It makes sense to change your career choice early on if you are not convinced by it.
4. A degree in a particular subject doesn't mean that only one avenue is open to you. For example, many students, after completing medical school, pursue careers in research, hospital administration or medical insurance.
5. Be mindful of your interests, passion, acumen, experience and finances.
6. Having a few guides and role models help, but having too many opinions is usually more confusing. Career counsellors are available to help.
7. If unsure, try and spend time as an observer in your profession of interest and try to know the struggles, challenges and rewards of that particular profession.
8. Sometimes, it makes sense to go with the flow. Don't be too hard on yourself.

12

THE QUESTION OF MONEY

'A penny saved is a penny earned.'

—BENJAMIN FRANKLIN

Money matters, and anybody who tells you that this is not true is lying. But what you do to acquire it and what you do with it is also equally important. Charles A. Joffe said, 'It's not your salary that makes you rich; it's your spending habits.' A Jamaican proverb goes further, 'Save money, and money will save you.'

Jatin had always wanted to become an engineer and worked hard towards it. He is a hard worker and got into a Fortune 500 company with an excellent pay package. Although he is getting paid better than most of his peers, the number of hours he is expected to put in has increased. He feels tired all the time and finds it difficult to meet deadlines as he works on unreasonable timelines.

He continues to work hard but has started making music on weekends which he had a passion for as a kid. This has brought back some joy and energy back into his life.

A salary or income is basically compensation for your time. Your time can be divided into personal, professional and social. If you focus too much on your professional life, then your personal and social life gets affected. How much personal and social time a person wants to sacrifice is an individual's choice and is not always in one's control.

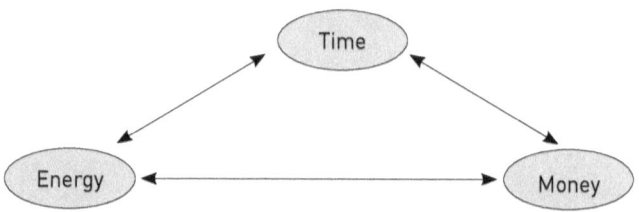

Figure 17: The interdependence of time, money and energy

Look at the picture carefully. If you can only have two of those, which ones will you choose, and why?

As children, one would have time and energy but no money; as working adults, one has money and energy but no time; and as one gets older, there is time and money but no energy. The constant endeavour to achieve a better balance between all three may lead to restlessness and dissatisfaction with life. Now, of course, there may be people who strike gold and are able to get all three, but then the worry about holding on to their name, lifestyle and social standing comes in.

Therefore, it is essential to understand money and materialism to ensure that one's personal and social life don't get impacted as one's career grows. It is further necessary to be able to make money grow with lesser efforts by saving and investing early on in life.

Making money sometimes seems easy; we feel that our unique idea to make it big will be successful. However, it is not just about the concept but also about correctly implementing it, and having the right resources and support make all the difference.

Success is also about adaptability and sustainability in the long run. Take Nokia, for example. A telecom giant that ranked 85 in the 2009 Fortune Global 500 listing and is now down at 485. Another case is that of Kodak, which was the market leader for everything in the photography industry in the twentieth century and had to file for bankruptcy in 2013. Therefore, planning for the future becomes more prudent as things may change very quickly unexpectedly.

The Basics of Money

It is possible that students of science or the humanities may not have any exposure to banking matters and terminology until they start earning in their early- to mid-20s. For example, 'debit' is the money that goes out of the bank account, and 'credit' is the money that comes into a bank account.

Having banking services and the option to invest at your fingertips (through your smartphone) makes it highly convenient, but at the same time, so many options make it confusing and more challenging.

An excellent place to start thinking about money is budgeting. We all hear about the national budget presented on 1 February every year. Similarly, your parents handle the household budget. It is equally important to manage your pocket money better by allocating money for things you need.

Try and save a little bit for a rainy day; even saving a little at a time helps learn and understand finance. You may save some money for yourself, ask your parents to open a bank account for you or choose some of the investment options described in subsequent pages. Do remember that while no investment is small, it is essential that one makes a start.

Bank Accounts

Every person should have a bank account. This helps develop a credit history or a credit score. Having a good credit score helps one avail loans and credit cards easily in the future.

There are several types of bank accounts available and the most common ones are described below:

1. **Savings Account:** It is a regular deposit account where you also get some interest on the money deposited. While different countries have different rules and ages at which minors can use banking services independently, most banks have the facility for saving accounts for minors.
2. **Current Account:** It is used by businesses and self-employed people. There are usually more frequent transactions in this account, and the interest rate is much lower.
3. **Fixed Deposit Account:** In this account, often referred to as an FD account, people can put an amount of money for a specified period for a fixed interest rate. The interest rate is usually more than the savings account, but there may be a penalty on breaking the fixed deposit earlier than term time.

Generally, when you open a bank account, you would be provided with a debit card, passbook and cheque book. You would also have the option of using Internet banking or net banking.

Net banking has made it much easier to avail banking services; it saves time and is convenient. Passbooks are being used less and less these days, but you may hear your parents or grandparents talking about them. Before the advent of digital banking, the passbook was a document that kept a list of the credit and debit transactions in your account. Cheques are personalized payment slips that you give to your creditors (people you owe money to), and they can go to the bank and withdraw money from your account by presenting those cheques.

Electronic Payments

1. **Debit cards** are payment cards linked to your savings or current account. When you use them, money gets deducted from the account balance instantly. Therefore, you can only spend money that you already have. Debit cards can be used to withdraw money from your own account at a authorized bank ATMs, make digital payments online and make payments at a retail store when making a purchase.
2. **Credit cards** are payment cards issued by financial institutions that let you borrow funds while adhering to a pre-approved limit to pay for your purchases. The limit is decided by the institution issuing the card based on your credit score and history.

    A credit card allows you to borrow money to make basic transactions, which are reflected on your bill; the bank pays the merchant immediately, and later, when you receive your credit card bill, you pay the bank. You should use a credit card only if you can pay the balance off in full each month.

It is all too easy to slide into credit card debt, which could give you the burden of paying off credit card debt as well as other loans. Credit card loans tend to charge 24–36 per cent interest. Plus, delaying your credit card payments affects your credit history, which could make it difficult to buy a car or a home or even get a job (in overseas countries). Sometimes, prospective employers check credit scores.

3. **Digital payments** in the form of payment wallets have become very popular. Payment wallets generally work like a debit card; you have first to add money to your digital wallet before using them.

Investments

Investments are extremely important for one's future, and it is vital to start your portfolio of investments as early as possible. Investments can essentially be thought of in terms of volatility—low risk with less percentage of return on your investment and high risk with higher return.

1. **Fixed Deposits**: The simplest form of investment where you invest a sum of money over a period of time for a fixed interest rate. Revisit the 'Fixed Deposit Accounts' section to refresh your memory.
2. **Public Provident Fund (PPF) account**: The PPF is a popular long-term investment option offered by the

Government of India that offers a high degree of safety to investment capital. You also get to earn interest at an attractive rate and reap returns that are fully exempted from taxation. A PPF account can also be opened in the name of an eligible minor. A minimum deposit of ₹500 to a maximum of ₹150,000 per financial year is allowed.

3. **Mutual Funds**: Money pooled in by many people (or investors) is what makes up a 'mutual' fund. A professional fund manager manages this fund. It is a trust that collects money from several investors who share a common investment objective. Then, it invests the money in equities, bonds, money market instruments and other securities. Each investor owns units, which represent a portion of the holdings of the fund. The income/gains generated from this collective investment is distributed proportionately amongst the investors after deducting certain expenses. Investments in Mutual Funds can also be done in a minors name and have to be linked to the minors' bank account.

4. **Shares**: Shares are small units of ownership that a person can buy from a large company or financial organization. Initial Public Offering (IPO) is the first-time shares that a company offers when they launch in the stock market and, subsequently, their shares can be traded. If the company is doing well, the share prices go up and if you sell, you make a profit on your investment. Even if you hold the shares and the company is in profit, they pay you a dividend. But the share prices can fall if the company is not doing well and the value of your investment can drop. To start trading in shares, one needs to have a Demat Account that can easily be opened through any bank.

5. **Cryptocurrency:** This is another high volatility investment. Cryptocurrency is entirely digital and has no physical form. It is a medium of exchange, and its legality varies from country to country.
6. **Global Investing**: India contributes to 3 per cent of global GDP. So, by investing only in India, one misses out on the growth opportunities available in the rest of the world. We consume the products and services of companies like Netflix, Apple, Google, Amazon, Samsung, etc., and hence it is crucial to participate in the wealth created by these business entities. International platforms make global investing very easy for investors in India without requiring them to commit a large amount of capital.
7. **Investment in property**: Investment in property remains a prominent investment option. Again, where you invest and how long you invest for can make a significant difference in the outcome. Whatever profit you make on a property deal is subject to a capital gains tax.

Taxation

Everyone has to pay tax in one way or another. Taxes are essential for the government. With the taxes collected, it manages the country's infrastructure, law and order, health care, education, defence, etc. There are two types of taxes that a person pays: direct tax and indirect tax. Direct tax includes taxes like income tax that everyone above a certain income per annum has to pay to the government. Indirect taxes include taxes like VAT and GST. Certain investments, like PPF and some investments in life insurance policies, are not subject to tax on income.

So, in a way, almost everyone in the country is paying tax in one way or another. At the end of the financial year, people file an annual return of their income and pay income tax on whatever they have earned over the exempted limits. Each country allows a certain amount of money that they can earn tax free and over that exempted limit they need to pay a tax to the government.

Insurance

Insurance has become essential in current times. Two insurances, which include life insurance and health insurance, are considered crucial. Insurance is relatively expensive and may seem like an added financial burden, but they can be beneficial at times of misfortune. There are added income tax benefits when people buy life and health insurance, and some life insurances also work like investments and pay a lump sum amount when people reach 60 years of age.

Loans

Loans are beneficial and, if used wisely, can help in personal and professional growth. Loans are money borrowed from financial institutions, and you have to pay it back with an added interest rate over time. The rate of interest and duration of time is already specified before you take the loan. Not paying the loan on time can affect your credit score, so it is essential to think about it thoroughly before taking this option. Most loans are secured, so you have to put something up as collateral to the financial institution, like a property against which they can give the loans. Credit card loans and student loans are considered unsecured as these are given based on your credit rating and future potential to pay them back. When you take a loan, you have to pay an EMI (equated monthly instalment) to pay the loan money back slowly.

Student loans are very important and helpful when students are going for higher studies. Generally, student loans have lower rates of interest than other types of loans and have extended repayment terms. The loan conditions are variable, and some student loans are given for a 15-year duration with no repayments/EMI until after one year of completion of studies.

Phishing

It is important to understand a little bit about phishing, which is a cybercrime and is fairly prevalent. Phishing entails people reaching out to you via email, voice calls or SMS, while posing as legitimate institutions and asking for money or your financial details like credit card numbers, passwords or account numbers.

This can lead to financial loss and identity theft. Always think twice about believing someone on the phone or email before providing any details. Most of the offers scammers give are too good to be true and are urgent or 'time sensitive'. If you are not sure, seek help from adults or call the institution yourself to check the validity of the offer before divulging any details.

Key points to consider:

1. Think of budgeting early in life. Ask your parents about how they do it.
2. Always try and save a portion of your allowance.

3. Ask your parents to open a bank account for you as soon as possible.

Five tips for parents:

1. **Teach your kids about budgeting:** An allowance can be a significant first step in showing your kids how to manage money. You might give money every week to the youngest children, at two-week intervals for preteens and monthly to teenagers. Gradually expanding the gaps between the time when money is given to them will help your children understand the need to manage their spending.
2. **Show them the value of saving:** It's only natural for the money to burn a hole in the pockets of the youngest kids. But they need to discover the benefits of delayed gratification. If there's a toy or a game that they have their eyes on, suggest they forgo spending their allowance on ice cream or another immediate pleasure and instead save for a few weeks to make the more significant purchase.
3. **Set savings goals for them:** To a kid, being told to save—without explaining why—may seem pointless. Helping children define a savings goal can be a better way to get them motivated. If they know what they want to save for, help them break down their goals into manageable bites. For example, if they're going to buy a ₹20,000 video game console and currently get a ₹500 allowance every month, help them figure out how long it will take to reach that goal, based on their saving rate.
4. **Provide a place to save their money:** Once your children have a savings goal in mind, they will need a place to stash their cash. This may be a piggy bank for younger kids, but if they are a little older, you may set up their own savings

bank account. That way, they can see how their savings are adding up and how much progress they're making toward their goal. Let them accompany you to the bank when you deposit the money collected in the piggy bank. Encourage them to fill a bank deposit slip after watching you do it a few times.

5. **Let them earn a little extra:** You probably expect your kids to clean their room, help with the dishes and do other daily chores. But consider offering them the chance to make extra money by helping to water the garden, wash the car or take on another job that goes beyond the routine. Getting paid for additional work will help instil good habits and give the children more control over saving and spending.

In conclusion, money is essential, but using it wisely remains a difficult skill to master. Do you go for instant gratification or reap the benefits in the long term? Having a good understanding of money matters, and having the support of an experienced financial analyst can help you and the money go further.

KEY POINTS

1. It is important to learn about money from an early age.
2. Parents should teach children the importance of money and the importance of saving money.
3. Take children to the bank, help them open a bank account and show them how to use an ATM.
4. If the children are mature enough, let them participate in discussions of family finances.
5. It is better to start investing sooner in life.
6. It is better to use cash, debit card or electronic wallet rather than a credit card.

Part 4

ADDICTIONS

'I think that no matter what you're doing as a teenager, you're going to be presented with peer pressure.'

—SARA PAXTON

13

INTERNET AND SCREEN ADDICTION

*'FOMO (Fear of missing out) is the
enemy of valuing your own time.'*

—ANDREW YANG

Take a minute to think about your Internet usage.

- How much time do you spend on the Internet every day?
- What do you look at on the Internet—study-related material, entertainment or social media?
- Does your Internet use adversely affect you or your relationships?
- Has your family commented on your excess Internet usage?
- Do you think you may be able to reduce your usage a little bit?

Ranil and Lata came to the outpatient department to discuss their four-year-old son, Ishan. They reported that they introduced Ishan to the iPad when he was three years old to teach him about animals, the alphabet, nursery rhymes and cartoons. The child seemed to enjoy it a lot and picked up information pretty fast. The parents also liked the iPad as a learning aid. He appeared very absorbed in front of the iPad. But soon, the parents noticed that he would be reluctant to leave it and would spend most of his time with it. It was becoming difficult for Ranil and Lata to engage his attention in anything else. Besides, they noticed tantrums when they took the device away from him. They panicked and reached out for help when they saw anger issues developing which they thought were related to the iPad use. They wondered if the four-year-old was addicted.

According to Mandy Saligari, giving your child a smartphone is like 'giving them a gram of cocaine'.[22] She said this at a conference in 2017, while highlighting the perils of gadgets for children and adolescents.

The Internet has profoundly affected our everyday experiences, becoming an integral part of modern life. It is seen as a boon to humanity and permeates all aspects of our lives. Several activities are performed on the Internet, both work-related and personal: surfing, emailing, downloading, social networking, blogging, navigating, gaming, chatting, etc. However, the Internet is not without its problems and Internet addiction is on the rise.

The first reports regarding excessive use of computers date back to the 1970s and 1980s. It was in the 1990s that the Internet was considered a tool that could lead to addiction. Dr Mark Griffiths (1995) included 'Internet use' as one of the

---

[22]Pells, Rachael, 'Giving Your Child a Smartphone Is Like Giving Them a Gram of Cocaine, Says Top Addiction Expert', *The Independent*, 7 June 2017, http://tinyurl.com/ywm4a6bf. Accessed on 3 January 2024.

many behaviours that could lead to a 'Technological Addiction'. He defined it as a non-chemical addiction involving human-machine interaction.[23]

The first to suggest addiction to the Internet was the American psychiatrist Ivan Goldberg. In 1995, he elaborated 'Internet Addiction Disorder'. However, it was Dr Kimberly Young who first investigated this disorder systematically.[24] Internet addiction is viewed as a behavioural addiction similar to gambling, shopping and eating.

Dr Kimberly Young views Internet addiction as an umbrella term for various behaviours divided into five subtypes.

1. **Computer addiction:** Obsessive computer game playing.
2. **Cyber relationship addiction:** Over-involvement in online relationships.
3. **Net compulsions:** Excessive online gambling, shopping or day trading.
4. **Information overload:** Compulsive web surfing or database searches.
5. **Cyber sexual addiction:** Compulsive use of adult websites for cybersex and cyberporn.

Features of Internet Addiction

Internet-addicted individuals report an inability to control their Internet use, which leads to feelings of distress and the impairment of daily activities. The basic features include:

---

[23]Griffiths, M.D., 'Technological Addiction', *Clinical Psychology Forum*, Vol. 76, 1995, pp. 14–19.

[24]Young, K.S., 'Internet Addiction: A New Clinical Phenomenon and Its Consequences', *American Behavioral Scientist*, Vol. 48, No. 4, 2004, pp. 402–15.

- Excessive use of the Internet beyond the allotted/intended time and being irresistibly preoccupied with the Internet
- Significant distress and impairment, mainly when the Internet is not available, or when the use has to be curtailed
- Increasing amounts of time spent on the Internet and the inability to cut down or stop Internet use
- Feeling restless, moody, depressed or irritable when attempting to cut down or stop Internet use
- Lying to conceal the extent of Internet use
- Compromising academics/work and social relationships because of Internet use

It is worthwhile to note that many similar behaviours are seen in other varieties of addictions.

Prevalence of Internet Addiction

International prevalence rates for Internet addiction have a significant variance depending on the measurement method and target population. A worldwide review reveals prevalence rates from 1.5 to 8.0 per cent for high school students. Compared to the rest of the world, Asian cultures have had the most significant problems with Internet addiction. Reported rates vary from 2 per cent to 20 per cent.[25] It is important to note that the diagnostic criteria for Internet addiction measurement are being continuously modified. The prevalence

---

[25]Yen, Cheng-Fang, et al., 'Internet Addiction: Ongoing Research in Asia', *World Psychiatry*, Vol. 9, No. 2, 2010, pp. 97, http://tinyurl.com/3e5f4ewr. Accessed on 3 January 2024.

rates continue to vary. But it is safe to assume that it is a problem for many across age groups.

Handheld gadgets like smartphones and tablets are becoming popular, with more and more people acquiring them at earlier ages.

Screen time is the amount of time spent using a device with a screen such as a smartphone, computer, laptop, television or video game console.

Children up to ten years of age have a screen time of about six hours, and children over ten years have screen times of nine hours a day or more.[26] Some children and teens may spend more time on devices than sleeping, eating, going to school or spending time with family and friends. Screen times likely increased significantly during the COVID-19 pandemic, and Internet addiction is now a threat in every household.

Some Startling Facts

The facts that follow have been compiled from various sources,[27] and the data seems to be ever-changing.[28]

- The average age when a child was exposed to screens in 2005 was four years of age; by 2012, it was four months old. This suggests that parents are providing access to

---

[26]'Screen Time and Children', *American Academy of Child and Adolescent Psychiatry*, 2020, http://tinyurl.com/3hbbb4du. Accessed on 3 January 2024.

[27]Lee, Hogan H., et al., 'Differences by Sex in Association of Mental Health with Video Gaming or Other Nonacademic Computer Use among US Adolescents', *Preventing Chronic Disease*, Vol. 14, 2017,
http://tinyurl.com/2zs2wubw. Accessed on 3 January 2024.

[28]Wong, Stephen, and Cass Dykeman, 'East Asians with Internet Addiction: Prevalence Rates and Support Use Patterns', Oregon State University, 2019.

gadgets to their children at a much younger age.

- A 2015 study from Pew Research Centre showed 59 per cent of girls and 84 per cent of boys in the age range of 13–17 years play video games. By 2018, more than 90 per cent of the children in the US were playing video games; 97 per cent of them were in the age range of 12–17 years old. Gaming addiction is widespread in this age group.
- South Korea may have up to 50 per cent of adolescents addicted to gaming. This is in line with the data that Internet addiction is more common in the Asian countries.
- 90 per cent of popular games portray violence. Some of the mass shootings in the US have been linked to video games.
- Excessive exposure to violent video games has been linked to aggressive behaviour later in life. It is particularly important for parents to understand that watching violent content must be avoided.
- Nomophobia, the fear of being without a cell phone or losing connectivity, is on the rise, and about 66 per cent of the population suffers from it. This is accompanied by intense anxiety and panic.
- In 2016, more than one-half of minors were being cyberbullied. One out of three reported cyberbullying threats.

Our attention spans have reduced since the advent of smartphones. Parents complain about poor concentration and high distractibility in children, and many children are now brought to clinics for evaluation.

The above data is ever-changing and varies according to countries, education, age groups, socio-economic status, etc. However, it conveys the penetration of technology/Internet in our lives, with dramatic negative consequences.

Health Effects of Internet Addiction

Internet addiction can have severe physical, psychological and social consequences in the short and long term.

Physical Effects

Light emitted from tablets screens and similar devices can cause melatonin suppression which affects our body's natural clock, making it harder for us to sleep. Melatonin is a hormone that is essential for maintaining the circadian rhythms of the body. This, in turn, has physical and psychological consequences, such as low mood, poor concentration, irritability, reduced performance, headaches and an increased risk of accidents.

As many as 95 per cent of individuals report using electronics in the hour before they go to sleep, which negatively impacts sleep.

Physical inactivity and spending less time outdoors lead to obesity and its consequences. Physical activity is vital for good health.

Headaches, eye strain and visual impairment have become more common and can be observed in young kids.

Repeated Strain Injuries (RSI) like neck and spine issues because of poor posture are seen more regularly. Carpal Tunnel Syndrome (CTS), a disease that affects one's wrists and was generally seen in middle age groups, has become more common because children are holding remote controllers or mobile phones in their hands for long periods of times in awkward positions.

Psychological Effects

The problems in attention, concentration and memory are leading to poor academic and work performance.

According to Steven Strogatz of Cornell University, 'Social media sites make it more difficult for us to distinguish between the meaningful relationships we foster in the real world and the numerous casual relationships formed through social media. By focussing so much of our time and energy on less meaningful relationships, our most important connections will weaken.' This is, unfortunately, already the case where the younger population has poor social connections and support, leading to social isolation.

J.M. Twenge's study of students in Classes 8, 10 and 12 in the USA looked for connections between happiness and screen versus non-screen activities.[29] The study revealed that adolescents' psychological well-being decreased as they spent more hours every week on screens. The unhappiest group were the teens who used screens more than 20 hours every week.

Instances of depression, anxiety, irritability and suicidal ideation are on the rise, along with risks of cyberbullying, stalking and being exposed to online predators.

Social Effects

---

[29]Twenge, Jean M. 'More Time on Technology, Less Happiness? Associations between Digital-Media Use and Psychological Well-Being', *Current Directions in Psychological Science*, Vol. 28, No. 4, 2019, pp. 372–79, http://tinyurl.com/399sw954. Accessed on 3 January 2024.

Addiction to the Internet is a major cause of damaged relationships. It dangerously affects the ability of people to have conversations in person. People feel more comfortable communicating through text messages rather than talking face to face.

This results in significant damage to relationships, and one may even lose touch with life and self. We gradually lose touch with loved ones, and isolation and loneliness begin to set in. This in turn may push individuals towards alcohol and drug use and also cause psychological problems such as anxiety, insomnia and depression. Over time, our brain chemistry may be altered, leading to more severe consequences.

Warning signs of technological addiction:

- Withdrawal from social relationships
- Isolation
- Neglecting important things
- Lying
- Lost sense of time
- Preoccupation with Internet use
- Emotional problems (anger/sadness)
- Poor academic performance
- Inability to control use/signs of dependency

Managing Internet Addiction

We must realize the benefits and pitfalls of technology and ensure that we use it to our advantage. An important question to ask is how much technology use is acceptable? While there cannot be a strict demarcation line, the American Academy of Pediatrics' (2016) recommendations for children's media use advises the following:

- **Children aged 2 or under:** Avoid all screen use except video calling with family.
- **Preschool kids:** Screen use should be limited to maximum one hour per day, and only for high-quality programmes.
- **Pre-teens and teens:** Don't let the use of screens/media impact other important activities like sleep, exercise, family meals and actively engage in 'unplugged time' like reading and board games.

What Can Parents Do?

It is incredibly distressing for parents to see their children get affected negatively by Internet dependence.

Parents should follow the Three M's model of parental involvement: monitoring, modelling and mentoring.

1. **Monitoring:** Openly communicate with children and help them understand the need for monitoring. We know that the Internet and social media can get a person in trouble. Hence, monitoring is essential. It is necessary to distinguish between monitoring and constantly hovering around the child, which can distress them.
   - Parents should know what children are doing online.
   - All technology use should be observable.
   - Consider placing filters and monitoring software on all gadgets.
   - 'Lights out, technology out.' Consider leaving devices out of bedroom at night.

2. **Modelling:** Parents are the first teachers and children emulate them. Parents need to display the behaviours that they expect the child to follow. There can be some rules for everyone in the household.
   - Do not use mobile phones while driving.
   - No technology at the dinner table.
   - No technology while interacting with family or socializing.
   - Limit your own screen time, both for your own health and as an example to your child.
3. **Mentoring:** This is very important as it leads to personal and professional development.
   - Parents should not be engaged in their own digital world all the time.
   - Build interests in children that are not digital.
   - Create a robust offline environment for children.
   - Help children structure their daily routines.

It's important to foster open and positive communication with children about technology use and safety guidelines. Permissive parenting (with too little control) or authoritarian parenting (with too much control and too little warmth) is counterproductive to the child's development.

Reading: The Wonder Drug

Reading books remains an important tool in improving focus, entertainment and removing people from the 'multi-tasking' mindset. It helps people focus better, improves vocabulary and helps give a break to the eyes while improving creative thinking. Try to read books from different genres and different authors. These give a different perspective towards life and helps to understand it better. Books can help one select careers, improve knowledge, develop lateral thinking, patience and, of course, help engage the mind in a positive manner. As George R.R. Martin said, 'A mind needs books as a sword needs a whetstone, if it is to keep its edge.'

The Internet represents a technological breakthrough, a new way of communication and a new era. The advantages of the Internet are numerous at both professional and social levels. However, we now know of its addictive potential. We need to understand that it cannot substitute the need for deeper interpersonal contact. It leads to faulty lifestyles with its consequences, especially for those who fall prey to its addictive potential.

We must aim to maintain a healthy relationship with technology and use it to our benefit, rather than becoming subservient to it.

KEY POINTS FOR PARENTS:

1. Have a healthy, open and trusting relationship with your child. This will go a long way in making the child feel secure. Be a role model for your children and engage in positive behaviours for your children to emulate.
2. Teach your children to never give out personal information such as their name, school, address, etc. Be wary of identifiable information in your child's profile.
3. Instruct your children never to plan a face-to-face meeting with an online acquaintance.
4. Establish clear rules for Internet use in the house (timings, not to use devices while eating or when guests are around, etc.)
5. The computer should be placed in a room that is open and

accessible to all family members. This way, the family will be able to monitor Internet use.
6. Encourage the use of a computer more than a handheld device.
7. Only people known and close should be befriended on social media. Friend requests from strangers should never be accepted.
8. Parents should be aware of the people on their child's friend list. Ask your child briefly about their friends.
9. Install reliable Internet filters and monitor your child's privacy setting on devices and social media accounts.

14

ALCOHOL USE

'Drunkenness is nothing but voluntary madness.'

—SENECA

Amit is a 16-year-old boy who went to a party with his older brother, who is 19. At the party, almost everyone was drinking alcohol. His brother's friends asked him to drink beer, which he refused at first but relented after some time. He felt judged, outdated and looked down upon when he refused alcohol.

The above experience is very true and familiar. The initiation almost always happens either from peer pressure or the feeling of being judged as backward. Of course, some people are curious and want to give it a go, but alcohol has become the go-to thing for any occasion.

According to the World Health Organization, about 16 per cent of the world's population uses alcohol regularly. Alcohol serves different purposes in a person's life. It is used for socializing, to look cool and fit in, to relax; some people use it to help them sleep. Heavy or problematic alcohol use is responsible for around three million deaths, severe disability and other illnesses in millions of other people.[30] It is therefore essential to reflect on the effect of alcohol in one's life.

What Is the Safe Limit?

Recent studies suggest that there are no safe drinking levels. Furthermore, 'low risk' drinking levels have been reduced to 14 units a week from previous 21 units.

This is how alcohol units are calculated:

3 Units	1 pint of beer or 568 ml (4–5 per cent)
	200 ml of wine (12 per cent)
	30 ml of whiskey (40–50 per cent)
	30 ml of vodka (40–50 per cent)

These 14 units should also be spread over 3–4 sittings and not consumed in one go. This is to reduce harm to the body both in terms of physical and mental health.

Alcohol use can be categorized into four types:

1. **Social use**: An adult drinking less than 14 units a week, which are also spaced out in 3–4 sessions
2. **Binge drinking**: A pattern of drinking more than five drinks in less than two hours for males and more than four drinks for females.[31] Binge drinking causes significant health and safety risks and can lead to subsequent dependence.

---

[30]'Alcohol', *World Health Organization*, 2022, http://tinyurl.com/hzxv2cmr. Accessed on 3 January 2024.

[31]Berridge, Virginia, et al., 'Binge Drinking: A Confused Concept and Its Contemporary History', *Social History of Medicine*, Vol. 22, No. 3, 2009, pp. 597–607, http://tinyurl.com/yb62xth7. Accessed on 3 January 2024.

3. **Harmful use of alcohol**: This is a stage where alcohol has become more regular. Despite the health impact, the person cannot cut down and ends up drinking more than 14 units per week or continues drinking despite major medical illnesses.
4. **Alcohol dependence:** A pattern of drinking where a person cannot go through their day without alcohol. They start drinking more and more in terms of quantity, start drinking during the day, have significant health challenges and experience alcohol withdrawals (shakes, sweats and restlessness) if they don't drink.

There are several risk factors and causes for alcoholism, including genetic, environmental and social causes.

A young person is at an increased risk if they:

1. **Experience peer pressure**: Young people have an inherent desire to fit in with the crowd and don't want to miss out.
2. **Engage with popular culture:** Young people are easily influenced by what they see on television, in films and music videos.
3. **Have low self-esteem:** Alcohol is falsely considered a confidence booster.
4. **Going through significant stressors:** Alcohol is considered a maladaptive coping strategy used to deal with stress as it generally increases long-term problems.
5. **Family culture:** Young people are more likely to abuse alcohol where there is excess use of alcohol at home.

Alcohol is known to cause physical, mental and social difficulties. Alcohol affects the liver, heart, causes neurological issues, weakens the immune system, worsens existing diseases and increases the likelihood of mouth, throat, liver, oesophagus, colon and breast cancer.

Unfortunately, it is used by many people as a coping mechanism to deal with stress, mental disorders and poor sleep. Alcohol is a known depressant and affects sleep adversely. It further reduces the efficacy of the medicines that a person may be taking to deal with mental or physical diseases. Stress is, therefore, actually worsened by alcohol and, so, must be avoided. While it can help one nod off to sleep and gives a deeper sleep during the first half of the night, it can, in the second half, cause more broken sleep, which leaves the person feeling unrefreshed in the morning.

Not only that, but the financial burden of alcohol is very high, and it can affect the social structure of the family. The economic cost is not just of the drink itself but also the treatment of various health issues related to alcohol, along with a major loss in productivity. Alcohol increases impulsivity, and there are more chances of legal problems for people with increased alcohol use.

Atul started using alcohol socially when he was 18 years old. His father liked to drink, and Atul would join him. After finishing graduation, Atul launched a start-up; after initial success, the start-up did not do as well as he expected. He started drinking to manage his mood and sleep. His girlfriend disapproved of his drinking and their relationship broke apart. He became more reckless and started gambling and lost his money.

His doctors and parents had to forcefully check him into a rehabilitation facility for his physical, emotional and social well-being.

How Can a Person Find Out if They Have an Alcohol Problem?

The CAGE questionnaire is used to screen people for alcoholism. It consists of four questions:

1. Have you ever felt that you should **c**ut down on your alcohol use?
2. Have people **a**nnoyed you by criticizing your drinking?
3. Have you ever felt bad or **g**uilty about your drinking?
4. Have you ever used alcohol as an **e**ye-opener to steady nerves in the morning?

A score of two or more means that it is an issue that needs attention and they must change habits.

Further signs of harmful alcohol use are drinking alone, eating poorly, ignoring personal hygiene, avoiding coursework, making excuses to drink and giving up on social and recreational activities because of alcohol use.

It may be possible for family members to pick up early signs of addiction. Some danger signs are:

1. Loss of interest in routine activities, hobbies and personal appearance
2. Declining school grades and difficulties in the school
3. Memory lapses, coordination problems, bloodshot eyes and unclear speech
4. Mood swings
5. Change in relationships with friends

What can a person do if they think they have an alcohol problem?

We would typically assess where a person lies based on the motivational interview cycle.

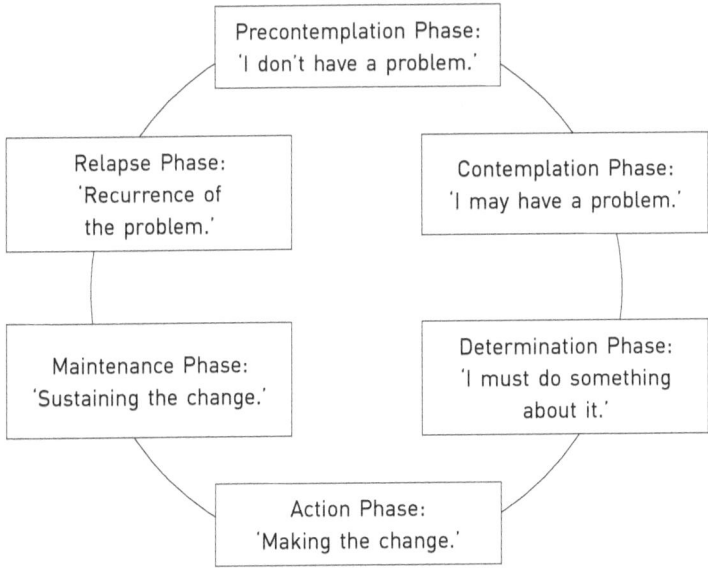

Figure 18: The motivational interview cycle

Acknowledging the issue is winning half the battle. If a person does not accept that they have a problem, it makes it that much harder to help them. It is essential to guide people towards the determination and action phase by educating them about the effects and side effects of alcohol use.

It is essential that the person takes ownership of the decision to change and does it for themselves rather than under pressure, as they are likely to be more successful in this way.

This motivational cycle is true for any addiction and is essential when you are trying to bring about any behavioural change in yourself, whether it is to remedy anger issues or obesity. Sometimes after a lot of hard work and maintenance, the behaviour may come back, but such is life. It is important to start again and not give up.

Rachita is 20-year-old and has often been told that she gets angry easily. She has never cared for it (pre-contemplation). On one occasion, she argued with her best friend after which her mother told her that she had been having a lot of angry outbursts with everyone around her. She found it hard to believe this and said that that was who she was and that she couldn't change. Later, she thought about what her mum said (determination) and spoke to her school counsellor (action), who offered to help her.

In summary, it would be complicated to ascertain if alcohol should have any role in modern society or not, as people use alcohol for different reasons. But if somebody has fallen into the alcohol trap, then they should know that help is available to quit or reduce alcohol use. It is very easily accessible, and awareness sessions need to start from school.

Families can set a good example by reducing their alcohol consumption and providing a supportive environment where young people can discuss the anxieties and challenges in their lives.

KEY POINTS

1. **Delay alcohol initiation** as much as possible. Alcohol is not compulsory in life, and you don't lose anything by not drinking.
2. **Seek help and support** as soon as you can from family and friends.

3. **Manage your stressors.** It is essential to identify the reason for alcohol use and deal with it.
4. **Engage better coping mechanisms.** Add exercise/hobbies/relaxation activities to manage day to day stressors.
5. **Counselling sessions can help.** This could be with a psychologist, counsellor or psychiatrist.
6. **Detox and rehabilitation:** People who have been drinking heavily may be offered medication to manage withdrawals and may subsequently be advised to spend some time in rehabilitation centres to reduce chances of relapse.
7. **Anti-craving therapy:** There are medications available that reduce the craving for alcohol, and they may be advisable for certain patients.
8. **Avoid alcohol cues.** Once off alcohol, avoid meeting people or going to places associated with alcohol use.
9. **Recurrence:** Don't despair if you start consuming alcohol again. Addictions have their ups and downs. Even if you restart alcohol, try again and focus on the reasons why the relapse happened and use it as a learning curve for the future.

15

NICOTINE ABUSE

'With a cigarette in my hand, I felt like a man.'

—Gary Lawyer

Ritesh is a 16-year-old boy who is fascinated by action movies. In his childhood he would dress up as an actor. He idolizes a few actors and wouldn't miss any of their films. He has grown up seeing his favourite actor smoke a cigarette and romance the female actresses. He has seen his older brother smoke a 'shisha' and has wondered what the big fuss was about smoking.

One day, he sees a few classmates with a vape and gives it a go for fun. He soon becomes hooked onto the vape as it was easy to hide and nobody at home could know about it.

The story sounds common enough and is entirely true. I think most young people have seen their favourite actors smoke on screen, and that doesn't set a great example for them as it normalizes or even glamorizes smoking. In India, both chewed and smoked tobacco are very readily available. The legal age when people can buy cigarettes in India is 18, but that has not been easy to enforce.

Nicotine is the key component of both cigarettes and chewed tobacco. According to the WHO, in 2015, about 1.1 billion people were smoking tobacco which is about one in six people; the data says that, in India, about 20.4 per cent of all adult males (>15 years age) smoke tobacco.[32] This proportion will be much higher than one in five if we include chewing tobacco too.

Nicotine is, in a way, a gateway drug—it can lead to the use of harder and more poisonous substances later in life.

There are several reasons why young people start using nicotine.

1. **Social pressure**: This remains the single most common reason for smoking. Young people have an inherent need to blend in and not feel left out. Nicotine use starts at an earlier age than before, and the desire to fit in with peers leads people to try it. It is an incredibly addictive substance. Subsequently, the use of the substance goes up and dependence builds.
2. **Social mimicking**: Young people are easily affected by what they see on social media and popular media like television, music videos, films and web series. If a role model/actor is seen smoking, it becomes easy to get influenced.
3. **Home mimicking**: The children in households where smoking or chewing tobacco is prevalent are more likely to pick up smoking.
4. **Stress**: Stress is the most common reason for people who start smoking a little later. Smoking is considered a maladaptive coping mechanism as it makes problems

---

[32]'Tobacco', World Health Organization, http://tinyurl.com/3d667ztu. Accessed 07 Dec 2023

worse rather than better. Working people smoke to counter stress, to distract themselves or to fight boredom and break the monotony of the day.

Tobacco is a killer, and young people continue to smoke despite knowing this. According to research done in the USA (by the FDA), about 2,000 new users try smoking cigarettes daily and about 300 become regular smokers each day.[33]

The Effects of Nicotine Use

Tobacco can affect physical health, mental health and also land a person in financial difficulty.

Smoked or chewed tobacco contributes directly to the death of half of its users. About eight million people die because of smoking every year; out of these, seven million deaths occur due to the direct effect of tobacco and 1.2 million deaths occur due to second-hand smoke. About one in five deaths in America are directly attributable to smoking, making it the single most significant preventable cause of death. This death rate is more than HIV-related, road traffic-related, firearm-related, alcohol and illicit drugs-related deaths combined.[34]

There are about 600 ingredients in a cigarette, and it creates about 7,000 different chemicals on burning. At least 70 of

---

[33]'Health Effects of Cigarette', *Smoking and Tobacco Use*, Centers for Disease Control and Prevention, 2021, http://tinyurl.com/4axjkmh6. Accessed on 3 January 2024. ; 'Cigarettes', U.S. Food and Drug Administration, http://tinyurl.com/3vsbf2bd. Accessed on 7 Dec 2023.

[34]'Tobacco', *World Health Organization*, 2023, http://tinyurl.com/yksb8c3r. Accessed on 3 January 2024.

these chemicals are known to cause cancer. The ingredients include arsenic (rat poison), tar (used to make roads), toluene (used to manufacture paint), naphthalene (used in mothballs), alongside nicotine. The assumption that chewing or inhaling tobacco is safe is also a myth. Chewing tobacco has around 28 different cancer-causing agents.

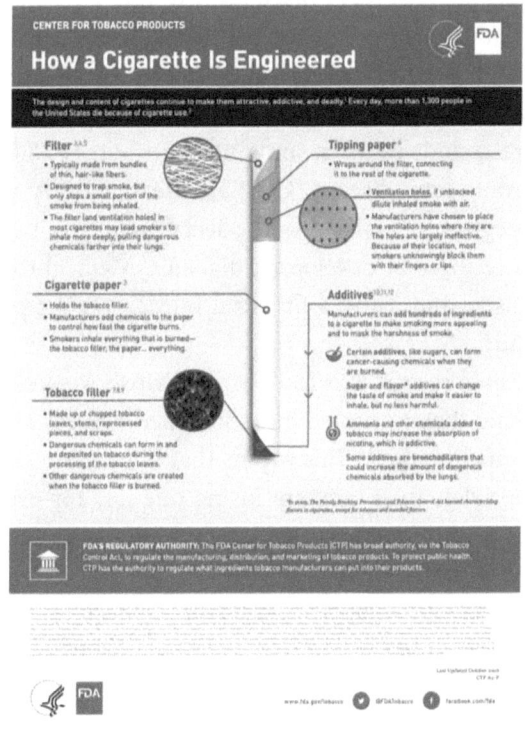

Figure 19: How a cigarette is made.[35]

---

[35]Center for Tobacco Products, 'How a Cigarette Is Engineered'. U.S. Food and Drug Administration, 24 April 2019. http://tinyurl.com/4xc4xsux. Accessed on 4 January 2024.

Cigarette smoking affects nearly all the organs in the body; it increases the risk of heart diseases and heart stroke by two to four times more than non-smokers. Smoking increases the chances of lung cancer by 25 times; smoking even fewer than five cigarettes per day increases the risk of heart disease. It increases the chances of lung cancer by 25 times.[36] It is also a well-established fact that tobacco contributes to cancers of the urinary bladder, stomach, liver, pancreas, larynx, certain blood cancers and gynaecological cancers, etc. Chewing tobacco further adds cancer of the tongue, lips, cheek and pharynx. Even if we exclude cancers, smoking contributes to 80 per cent of all chronic lung disease (COPD), affects fertility in males, affects pregnancy, causes tooth decay, weakens bones and increases chances of developing diabetes. Medical treatments are expensive and cause a financial burden on the person or their family.

Published research in 1999 in the British Medical Journal (BMJ) found that every cigarette consumed reduces 11 minutes of a person's lifetime.[37] This means that if a person smokes 20 cigarettes a day, then they are losing one day for every week of smoking, and smokers, on average, die 6.5 years earlier compared to non-smokers.

Moreover, nicotine has an adverse effect on a person's mental health—nicotine, being a stimulant substance, disrupts sleep and increases anxiety and heart rate. It also reduces the

---

[36]'Health Effects of Cigarette Smoking', *Centers for Disease Control and Prevention*, 2021, http://tinyurl.com/4axjkmh6. Accessed on 3 January 2024.
[37]Shaw, M, et al., 'Time for a Smoke? One Cigarette Reduces Your Life by 11 Minutes', *BMJ (Clinical Research Ed.)*, Vol. 320, No. 7226, 2000, pp. 53, http://tinyurl.com/3w2pha7p. Accessed on 3 January 2024.

impact of medications that a person may be on. Cigarettes/tobacco are also a financial drain on a family, with funds going towards the procurement of substances rather than on the family's welfare.

How can one quit smoking?

1. **Fix up a date** to quit.
2. **Get support.** This could be from family members, friends, counsellors or doctors. Tell them not to offer cigarettes or vapes and not to smoke in front of you.
3. **Identify your stressors** and try and sort them out as best as you can. It is harder to quit if you are distracted or restless because of ongoing stressors.
4. **Be proactive** and add better coping mechanisms. Try to add exercise or hobbies to your day. This will ensure better tolerance to stress and increase the positivity of mood.
5. **Avoid smoking cues.** Avoid people and places that remind you of smoke.
6. **Seek professional help.** Medications in the form of Nicotine Replacement Therapy (NRT's) and anti-craving therapy are available. Your doctor would be able to suggest what will be best for you.
7. **Seek counselling.** Having frequent motivation-boosting appointments with a therapist increases one's chances of quitting.
8. **Don't be disheartened.** Addictions, unfortunately, follow a cycle to relapse and remission, which means that a lot of people will frequently relapse before finally giving up the addiction for good. Even if you have relapsed, do not despair and try again.

Are E-Cigarettes Safe?

Electronic cigarettes are battery-operated devices that emit a vaporized solution to inhale. The solution has nicotine as its main component, but it still needs other additives to burn. It is also known as vaping. Initially, it was made available as a tool for cutting down or quitting smoking. But unfortunately, it became very popular with non-traditional smokers, and young people started getting addicted to it. Therefore, it has recently been banned in many countries around the world.

They contain nicotine and are a hazard to the health. They do not prevent second-hand smoking and may make quitting more difficult in some people. Experimental use by teens may be more dangerous, and can harm brain development while also causing difficulties in attention and learning in young people.

There is no safe level of tobacco use, and there is no perfect time to quit smoking. Your energy and sense of taste and smell will return within weeks or months of quitting smoking. The risk of strokes and heart disease reduces to that of a non-smoker after two to five years of quitting. The risk of lung and oral cancers reduce by 50 per cent within five to ten years of quitting.[38]

Even if you think you can't stop, cutting back on use will improve your health. A lot of help is available if a person is keen to quit smoking, however nothing helps if there is no motivation from within.

---

[38] 'Benefits of Quitting', Centers for Disease Control and Prevention, 2017, http://tinyurl.com/4we895w5. Accessed on 3 January 2024.

Cigarettes and another nicotine products are highly addictive, and despite the best initiatives of government agencies, the use of nicotine is increasing in developing countries. It is difficult to break the habit of smoking once one becomes addicted.

Needless to say, prevention is the best cure. There are numerous government and international agencies and awareness programs to stop young people from becoming addicted to smoking. You do not lose out on anything if you don't smoke.

KEY POINTS FOR PARENTS

If you find out about a possible addiction that your child has:

1. Be supportive.
2. Look for reasons/causes for the addiction.
3. Stress, mental disorders and peer pressure are common causes for addictions.
4. Some addictions have withdrawals and need gradual reduction or detoxing instead of abrupt cessation.
5. Addictions and mental disorders may need help concurrently.
6. Seek help sooner. Counsellors', psychologists' or psychiatrists' input could be vital.
7. Self-help groups can also lend a good sense of support.

16

DRUG ABUSE

'Addiction is the opposite of connection.'

—ANONYMOUS

Adolescence is a time where a lot of developmental changes happen in a person's life. It is also a time when people try to express their personalities, and sometimes the influence of peers can become quite pervasive in our lives. More often than not, the influence of peers is positive, as with them one finds acceptance, encouragement, feedback and advice. But sometimes, the influence can be harmful. Because people naturally want to 'fit in', they may find it difficult to resist the pressure to engage in particular activities.

19-year-old Tarang went to the Netherlands with his friends. He felt intrigued by the concept of hash brownies. He tried two brownies and had a couple of beers too. He slept well but, on waking up, he felt anxious and that his friends were against him and wanted to harm him. He hit his friends, and the police had to be called. He was admitted to a psychiatric unit with a diagnosis of drug-induced psychosis.

Most of the time, drug dependence, alcohol use and smoking start with peers' encouragement to try it. This, unfortunately, sets some people down the road of addiction that is difficult to escape.

Why Are Some Drugs Legal if They Are Not Safe?

Following the legalization of cannabis in some countries and the decriminalization of other drugs in some countries, there is a perception that certain drugs are harmless. Unfortunately, this is far from the truth.

There are reasons why governments have legalized and decriminalized certain drugs. In 1920, the National Prohibition Act was passed in the USA, which banned the manufacture and sale of alcohol. Although the rates of liver failure, alcoholic psychosis and infant mortality went down drastically, crime rates shot up. It gave rise to rum-running and bootlegging, where people started smuggling alcohol in their trouser legs. Thousands of people died by drinking unsafe alcohol. Therefore this act was eventually repealed in 1933, and since then, alcohol has been available legally.

Cannabis is considered an entry-level drug and considered a 'safer' drug compared to other hard drugs. There is a significant difference between the words 'safe' and 'safer', where the latter is a relative word meaning that it is less harmful compared to other drugs. For most people, it may not have a harmful impact. Still, the ones who experience the harmful effects can face a lifetime of anxiety, depression and other severe mental disorders like bipolar disorder and schizophrenia. Furthermore, the idea of legalizing cannabis especially is to reduce exposure to drug dealers who may entice young people towards harder drugs, and channel that money to terrorist activities, gang wars and human trafficking.

Cannabis

Cannabis, also known as marijuana, hash, pot, weed, ganja or hemp, is made from a plant known as *Cannabis sativus*. It is derived from dried flower buds, while Hash is a resin from the plant's sap. Hash contains a higher number of psychoactive substances.

Cannabis has several compounds, and these together are called Cannabinoids. Two of these are Tetrahydrocannabinol (THC) and cannabidiol (CBD), which are the most common cannabinoids found in cannabis products. Both THC and CBD interact with receptors in the brain that control pain, mood, sleep and memory. THC causes euphoria and, in extreme amounts, can cause paranoia, anxiety and panic, while CBD counterbalances the effect of THC and brings a feeling of well-being.

Unfortunately, there is now a high availability of synthetic and genetically modified cannabis, with a much higher THC-to-CBD ratio. These are stronger compounds without the counterbalance of CBD and, therefore, have a much higher risk of initiating anxiety and psychotic disorders.

Short term effects of sustained cannabis use include the impact on memory, comprehension and learning, increased heart rate, anxiety and paranoia. At the same time, chronic use can cause memory impairment, aggressive and rebellious behaviour, low motivation, psychosis and other mental disorders.

As mentioned earlier, there is no way to predict who is more vulnerable to the adverse effects of cannabis. Research has indicated a six-fold increased risk of schizophrenia in young people using heavy cannabis before the age of 18.[39] Cannabis specifically affects the frontotemporal areas of the brain, which affects the brain's memory, learning and motivation circuits. The effect can be seen in poor school performance, the need to work harder to achieve results and changes in behaviour in school and at home.

Cannabis, however, has been found to have some medicinal use in diseases like chronic pain and epilepsy, but the percentage of cannabinoids used in these cases is very specific and carefully calibrated to avoid any adverse effects.

Categories of Drugs

Furthermore, drugs can broadly be classified as stimulants, CNS depressants, sedatives and hallucinogens.

Stimulants or 'uppers' are drugs such as cocaine and amphetamines. Cocaine, also commonly known as coke, snow or white, is considered the 'rich man's drug'. The ease of administration makes it a widely used drug of abuse. Amphetamine, and the related methamphetamine (crystal meth), is also a popular drug. Stimulants produce a powerful and short-acting euphoria and alertness. They were initially considered harmless but were later found to be incredibly addictive, and users can move from recreational use to

---

[39] Andréasson, Sven, et al., 'CANNABIS and SCHIZOPHRENIA a Longitudinal Study of Swedish Conscripts', *The Lancet*, Vol. 330, No. 8574, 1987, pp. 1483–86, http://tinyurl.com/5ytnk57n. Accessed on 3 January 2024.

using several times daily within weeks. Users can develop insomnia, loss of appetite, financial issues, anxiety disorders and psychosis. Amphetamines have found a medicinal role in treating certain medical illnesses that have impaired concentration and excessive sleep as their primary symptoms.

Central Nervous System (CNS) depressants or 'downers' are drugs that cause sedation and numbness. The prime example of these classes of drugs is opiate derivatives. Opiates include heroin (brown, brown sugar, smack), certain painkillers and cough suppressants. These are some of the most addictive drugs and also the most physically harmful drugs available. They are lethal in big doses as they cause respiratory depression (slowing breathing) and have a bad withdrawal profile, causing the user to continue using them despite not wanting to.

Sedatives usually include sleeping tablets and certain antiseizure medication. The use generally starts as a treatment for anxiety or sleeplessness, but the tolerance soon develops and becomes a full-blown addiction. In contrast to other drug addictions, this addiction typically affects slightly older persons, compared to other addictions seen mostly in late teenage and early adult years. Sedative withdrawal is not dissimilar to alcohol withdrawal and is characterized by restlessness, lack of sleep, anxiety, tremors, sweating and panic.

Mudit was due to give his Class 10 board exams but was feeling very anxious. His brother, a medical student, advised him to take an anti-anxiety medication without any counselling. Mudit found immediate relief, and his exams went well. But since then, he feels that if he does not take an anti-anxiety medication, he can't do well and actively looks for them before exams.

Hallucinogens or party or rave drugs include drugs like MDMA and LSD. Their effects can range from bliss (feeling spaced out) to intense anxiety or terror (bad trip). These are not drugs that are used daily but usually only at parties. Excess use can cause psychosis and severe depression.

Everyone Does Them! Why Not Me?

No drug is considered harmless, and unfortunately, despite some people being able to tolerate some drugs in vast quantities, we do not have a way of accurately predicting what can cause harm and what doesn't cause harm. Each drug is considered psychoactive, which interferes with the brain's chemistry and processes like cognition, mood and thinking. The effect of these substances depends on a person's vulnerability (genetics and health), type of substance, amount, frequency of use and the purity of the substance. The effect on a person can be acute (immediate and for a short duration) or chronic, affecting a person's physical or mental health. Finally, the impact could directly affect one's health or indirectly affect one's professional performance and cause legal and/or financial problems.

What to do if you are addicted to drugs?

1. **Confide in someone you know and trust**: If you have realized that you have been taking drugs and are unsure what to do, reach out to a responsible adult who can guide you.
2. **Seek professional help**: You may reach out to a psychiatrist who can explore the reasons for use and advise you about a healthy way of coming off them. Some drugs can be

stopped straight away, but some have severe withdrawal effects. Sometimes the management of withdrawal is possible at home, but for severe addictions, they may need to be managed in dedicated hospitals.
3. **Don't give up:** Drug addictions have an up and down cycle. People become clean and then relapse again. Even if you have relapsed, try again with more help and support.
4. **Don't celebrate abstinence with the drug you were abstaining from**: There is nothing called 'controlled use'. Trying to celebrate with the same drug that one was abstaining from can kick-start the addiction again. This is true for all addictions, including cigarettes, alcohol and all drugs of abuse.

A child using drugs is also a challenging time for parents. This is an age group where children want to assert their independence and parents want to protect them from falling into bad habits. Change only comes from within; pressuring makes typically things more difficult.

KEY POINTS FOR PARENTS

Here are a few signs of addiction and some ways to help and support your child.
1. **Look for the change in behaviour**: Look for signs, such as irritability, financial irregularity, lying and change in the friend circle.
2. **Change in appearance**: Watch out for constant tiredness, red eyes, missing school and classes, staying out most days.
3. **School performance**: Has there been a drop in school grades?
4. **Support the child and look for reasons for use**: Sit with your child and figure out why they could have turned to using drugss.

5. **Seek professional help and support**: Your doctor should be able to guide you on the best way forward. This could also mean admission to a rehabilitation centre to reduce chances of relapse in future.
6. **Do not despair if the child has relapsed**: Start again. Sometimes it takes two to three cycles of relapse and remission to achieve complete abstinence.
7. **Set a good example**: Do not normalize substance abuse at home.

Drugs remain a curse to society. Selective abstraction of information and an incomplete understanding generally cause discord between parents or doctors and young people. Not trying drugs and understanding what drugs can and can't do to mental and physical well-being is extremely important.

KEY POINTS

1. No drugs are considered safe.
2. Once you start, it is incredibly hard to stop.
3. Certain drugs are called 'gateway drugs'. They increase the likelihood of using 'harder drugs', later in life.
4. Confide in an adult if you feel you have become dependent on drugs.
5. Change your friend circle if they pressure you to do drugs. Find friends who don't use any substances.
6. Increase physical activity as it helps keep dopamine levels high.
7. Self-help groups can provide good support to maintain abstinence.
8. Seek professional help to manage withdrawals.

17

COFFEE: THE WORLD'S FAVOURITE DRINK

'Coffee, the favourite drink of the civilized world.'

—THOMAS JEFFERSON

Who doesn't love a cup of hot coffee in the morning or a luxurious iced coffee in the summers. But why are we talking about it in this book, and especially in this section?

Could it be addictive?

Caffeine is used by most of the population in different forms and for different reasons. It is useful for socializing and also as a pre-workout booster before the gym or playing a sport. It is used to enhance one's concentration before important work, assignments, exams and, most commonly, as an eye-opener in the morning. About 90 per cent of adults in the USA consume some form of caffeine daily compared to about 16 per cent of people using alcohol worldwide, making caffeine the most commonly used legal psychoactive substance in the world.[40]

A cup of instant coffee has about 100mg of caffeine, a can of cola drink about 30mg and a cup of tea or green tea can also have about 30mg of caffeine. A caffeine-based energy drink has about 80mg of caffeine in each can. A caffeine pill has anywhere between 100-200mg in each tablet. You would be surprised to hear that even chocolate bars have caffeine and 100 grams of dark chocolate has about 43mg of caffeine.

Try and calculate your daily caffeine intake with the above figures.

So, we are all consuming caffeine, knowingly or unknowingly, in one form or the other. Caffeine as a substance has a long half-life of about five to six hours. Half-life refers to the time taken to reduce the concentration in your blood by half of the original consumption. Let's assume you consumed 100mg of caffeine at 8 a.m. By 2 p.m., you would have 50mg in your blood and by 8 p.m., about 25mg.

There is, of course, a cumulative effect—we keep drinking hot or cold beverages throughout the day either to improve concentration or fight boredom. Therefore, the amount of caffeine builds up in our system.

Now, let's say a man had a cup of coffee at 8 a.m., then another cup around 12 and then another about 5-6 p.m. By 11 p.m., which we can assume is time to sleep, he would still have more than 100mg of caffeine in his blood, which is the same as going to bed after drinking a fresh cup of coffee.

---

[40]Mitchell, Diane C., et al., 'Beverage Caffeine Intakes in the U.S', *Food and Chemical Toxicology*, Vol. 63, 2014, pp. 136–142, http://tinyurl.com/yc5xzwr6. Accessed on 3 January 2024.

Anuj loves his coffee and often drank 3-4 cups of coffee throughout his day. He is pursuing a PhD and, as he is inching closer to his submission date, feels the need to work harder and sleep less to finish his work. He started using caffeine tablets to stay awake for longer. After a few days of increasing coffee cups and taking three caffeine tablets, he found that he couldn't sleep at all despite wanting to. He also felt that his heartbeat was racing, and he couldn't sit at his desk. He visited a physician and had to be given sleeping tablets for a few days.

Caffeine, being a stimulant, delays sleep and wreaks havoc on one's sleep structure and makes the person feel droopy and sapped of energy in the morning. This starts the vicious cycle of having more coffee to feel alert which disrupts sleep again.

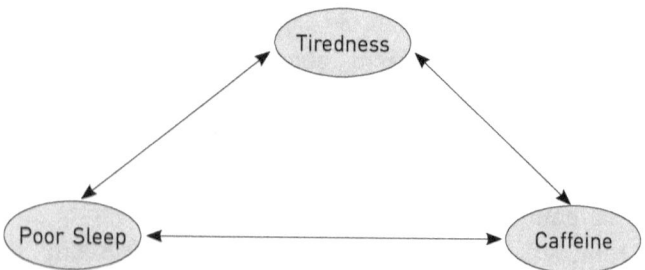

Figure 20: The coffee triad: a self-fulfilling prophecy

Of course, caffeine not only disrupts the sleep cycle but is also a well-known agent that can worsen anxiety disorders and restless legs syndrome. Together, these can have adverse effects on sleep.

Students take caffeine to stay up and study, which is a counterproductive strategy, as it only helps in the short term.

Still, the disruption in sleep quality and fatigue in the morning will reduce one's efficiency and productivity during the next day.

Caffeine is also a diuretic, which means it causes increased urination. Caffeine in excess can increase heart rate, and thus, those who have heart diseases should avoid consuming a lot of caffeine. It also has the potential to worsen anxiety disorders. People who already suffer from anxiety disorders and panic attacks should avoid caffeine entirely or consume it in moderation.

Most people feel that they can sleep well despite having a coffee late at night, but the changes in sleep structure often happen without the person consciously realizing it. The effects of this may not be visible if it is a one-off episode, but regular use would start impacting our energy levels and work performance.

It would be incorrect to say that we should stop consuming caffeine completely; as mentioned previously, coffee plays different roles in our lives, but we can definitely try to cultivate a healthier relationship with caffeine.

Anuj continues to love his coffee but has reduced his coffee cups to two a day and changed his coffee to the decaffeinated version.

There will, of course, be people who would have a better tolerance to caffeine than others, but most of the time, caffeine makes changes to our metabolism and sleep without us realizing it. Reducing caffeine improves sleep, making you feel fresher in the long run and improving your efficiency. This will help in the reduction of stress and improve productivity.

KEY POINTS

1. Try to reduce caffeine intake proactively.
2. Have your caffeine fix earlier in the day so that by the time you go to sleep, most of it has washed out of your system. Avoid coffee after 4–5 p.m.
3. Try and go without coffee for a month and assess your energy levels and judge for yourself whether going without coffee has had any adverse effects on your life.
4. If you can't cut down or stop coffee, try the decaffeinated coffee (which has about 1/10th of caffeine content compared to regular coffee). Keep in mind that it is usually more expensive than the normal variety.
5. Be mindful of caffeine content in other food products and drinks too.

Part 5

MIND MATTERS

'The mind is not a vessel to be filled,
but a fire to be kindled.'

—PLUTARCH

18

MENTAL HEALTH: LET'S NOT TALK ABOUT IT

'There is no health without mental health.'

—THE LANCET

Think of the times you have heard statements like:

1. Stress is nothing but a fad.
2. Pull your socks up and get on with it.
3. Do you think we didn't have any stress in our lives?
4. Stop making excuses. Look at the other person's problems; they are much bigger than yours.
5. Sleep it off, and you will be fine.
6. If they have everything then why are they sad or behaving this way?
7. This is such a small thing.

This is just a selection of what I get to hear in my clinic, but I am sure each one of us has heard these statements in our life. The proverb, 'A stitch in time saves nine,' has never felt truer. It is essential that we talk about mental health. The subjectivity and personal impact of stress on each individual must be understood.

As stress is increasing, so are the instances of mental disorders in the world. It is estimated that one in four of us will experience some mental health issues in our lifetime. In the adolescent population, it is estimated that 10–20 per cent (which is around 100–200 million out of 1.2 billion adolescents in the world) experience some mental health difficulties. Moreover, the onset of more than 50 per cent of adult mental health illnesses starts between 14–20 years of age. Therefore, it is essential to understand what mental health means and how to maintain good mental health.[41]

The stigma associated with mental illnesses remains the biggest hurdle in seeking help and ultimately leads to severe mental disorders and, in extreme cases, suicide. People tend to associate the word mental illness with insanity, which is incorrect. There are more than 100 types of mental illness, ranging from mild to severe. While severe mental conditions are relatively rare, mild to moderate ones are very common. Adequate and early detection of mental illnesses can prevent the development of severe mental disorders later in life.

Despite a strong public health campaign on mental health and the better availability of psychologists in schools, the lack of awareness, prejudice, cost, privacy and local availability of care remains a barrier to accessing mental health support services. Most young people have to rely on adults, including

---

[41]'The World Health Report 2001: Mental Disorders Affect One in Four People', *World Health Organization*, 2001, http://tinyurl.com/222vxajs. Accessed on 3 January 2024.

teachers and family, to recognize signs of mental illness and facilitate access to mental health care.

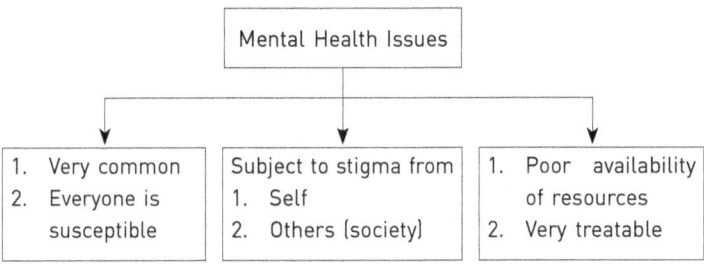

Figure 21: The different aspects of mental health

Why Do Mental Illnesses Happen?

There are several reasons why people develop mental illnesses. It is considered a complex interaction of genes and environmental factors. Unfortunately, not much can be done about genetics, but the environmental factors can be modified if they are identified early.

People with disabilities, those who suffer from chronic illnesses (diabetes, thyroid disorders, HIV), people who face stigma because of sexual orientation, ethnicity, economic status, caste, etc., and those exposed to violence, poverty and unloving households are more vulnerable to mental disorders. Children bullied for their weight, acne, hair loss and height are also susceptible to developing low self-esteem and low confidence that can lead to more severe mental disorders in later life. Mental health problems can affect anyone at any point of their lives. Stress is very personal and subjective. People seem to have 'perfect lives' from the outside but may be struggling internally. Professional and financial success does not preclude people from having mental disorders.

Sarah is a high school student and is constantly bullied because of her acne. Due to the bullying, she became more isolated and started using more make-up to cover her acne. She would avoid making eye contact with others and going to birthday parties. Her grades have dropped, and she cries herself to sleep. However, she is afraid to ask an adult or professional for help because she thinks her problems are insignificant compared to others and that she would be scolded for feeling this way.

Stigma

Stigma remains the foremost reason for the poor uptake of mental health support. The common notion that people can just 'pull up their socks' and get better, and the idea that people are just making it up remains a hurdle to seeking help and support.

We can divide stigma into two broad categories. The first one is the stigma from the family and society at large. People often think that they have been cursed or that they will tarnish the family name if they have a mental disorder. These reasons are commonly heard in clinics and at support group meetings. Families hesitate to associate with families that have members with mental disorders.

The other significant second is the shame that the person feels when they have a mental disorder. The notions of 'how can this happen to me?', 'I am strong', 'I am not stressed' are some things that a person says to convince themselves that they are okay. Acceptance and acknowledgement are the first steps towards recovery. It is safe to say that everyone remains vulnerable to developing mental illness in these times, and in order to lower the risk, we must take care of our physical and mental well-being.

Another myth is that mental disorders persist for a lifetime and are not treatable. Almost all mental illnesses are treatable, and most of them need help only for a few months.

Even the best athletes in the world—be it Cristiano Ronaldo, Virat Kohli or Usain Bolt—would need help if they injure themselves. It does not mean that they are weak, nor does it mean that they would be disabled for life. It is just that at some point, we all need the extra help and support.

Common Mental Disorders

Mental disorders are clinical illnesses which can only be diagnosed by professionals. There are diagnostic criteria which need to be fulfilled before a clinical diagnosis is made. These criteria include consideration of symptoms, their intensity and the duration that they have been experienced. The level of impact on one's day to day functioning is also considered. It is also important to rule out any other condition like neurological diseases, side effects of prescribed medicines, etc. before a diagnosis is confirmed.

Self-diagnosis and diagnosis made through Internet questionnaires can be incorrect and can have severe repercussions and should be avoided.

By far, the most common mental illnesses seen in adolescents is anxiety and depression.

Anxiety Disorders

Nikhil has been experiencing episodes of sweating along with a raised heartbeat and shortness of breath whenever he goes into a lift. He has been climbing 5–6 floors to avoid getting into the lift. He once got locked in an elevator a few months ago and since then has been avoiding lifts. One of these days, he refused to get into the car but was okay to travel by bike.

Anxiety disorders is a term that is commonly used for a variety of illnesses like Generalized Anxiety Disorder (GAD), panic attacks and phobias, among others. The core symptoms of anxiety are fear and apprehension, with physical symptoms like a fast heartbeat, feeling breathless, becoming sweaty and tense and a constant foreboding of something terrible going to happen.

Anxiety is the 'fight-flight-freeze' reaction of the body. Whenever the body finds itself in a challenging or stressful situation, it starts preparing itself. The heart starts beating faster; the lungs try to take in more air by breathing deeply, the blood supply to muscles increases and alertness improves—all these constitute physical symptoms of anxiety. Not all anxiety is terrible, and it may be similar to feeling butterflies in the stomach before exams or before opening a present. It is only an illness when one feels anxious either needlessly, disproportionately and/or in a sustained manner.

The person having anxiety issues can exhibit irritability, be avoidant and isolative, avoid eye contact and be restless. It is essential to have patience and support them in dealing with their anxiety. Anxiety is often accompanied by avoidance behaviours where we try to avoid problematic situations or situations that our mind deems as 'dangerous', an example of which is illustrated above.

Depression

Depression, as a word, has now moved into the common vocabulary. We all have our ups and downs, and we may remark that we feel low or depressed on a certain day. Clinical depression, however, includes the core symptoms of low mood and an inability to find joy in things. This is supplemented by symptoms of low appetite, lack of motivation, poor sleep, lack of interest in personal appearance, poor concentration, poor self-esteem and, in severe cases, suicidal thoughts. These symptoms need to be sustained for at least 14 days and be present in personal, social and professional life for them to be categorized as clinical depression.

We all feel low or distressed when things do not go our way; it is a natural reaction to personal setbacks. Being mindful of your feelings and trying to compensate with suitable coping mechanisms is essential to dealing with these situations faster so that they do not progress to clinical depression.

A person struggling with depression will appear relatively quiet, avoid interactions, have poor concentration, and be irritable. Their grades might be falling, and they might seem more emotional.

Akshay recently took his exams and did not do exceptionally well in them. He had not expected to do great, but unfortunately, he did not pass this time. He has been inconsolable for the last three weeks and pretends to be tired and asleep all day. He thinks he has let his family down and that he can never be a good son (hopelessness) and that nobody wants to see him (worthlessness). He also feels that nobody can help him now (helplessness).

As mentioned earlier, the person going through a depressive episode may not sometimes acknowledge it themselves and be actively against the idea of seeking help. They do, however, need extra support from friends, school and family around them. They need to feel that they are in a supportive environment where they can express what they are feeling, and they have to be supported with a lot of patience and encouragement. The help and treatment options available for any mental disorder have never been more readily available than they are now. The treatment options range from simple talking therapies (counselling or psychotherapy) to medications, depending on the person's symptoms.

Unfortunately, the availability of help and engagement with treatment remain poor. Even in developed countries where people are more aware of mental health disorders, the percentage of people who seek consistent treatment is low.

Bipolar Affective Disorder

Bipolar affective disorder is a severe mental illness that is characterized by people experiencing sustained mood swings. The mood changes can range from feeling depressed to having excessive energy, lack of sleep, impulsivity and increased productivity. Contrary to popular belief, bipolar affective disorder is only diagnosed when these mood swings are sustained over days and weeks. Regular ups and downs in mood according to circumstances are not bipolar.

Smita is a 15-year-old girl who generally used to be very shy, but she has been talking a lot over the last few weeks. She has been putting herself forward for every competition and extra-

curricular activity in school. She has scored low in her exam but doesn't seem bothered by her result and remains extra gregarious. She has been very boastful and has been making what appear to be impulsive decisions.

In this example, Smita has had a general change in behaviour lasting weeks, and her behaviour patterns are out of character for her usual self. The above changes can also be seen when people have a neurological condition, are using illicit drugs or as a side effect of some medications.

Schizophrenia

Schizophrenia is a type of psychotic illness where people experience paranoia and feel that other people are talking about them. It is associated with them experiencing auditory hallucinations (voices) that no one else can hear. It generally begins in adolescence, and early treatment can prevent a lifetime of difficulties.

Mayank is a 17-year-old boy who has suddenly become quiet and has reduced his interaction with others. He is often seen smiling without any reason and has been seen talking to himself. He is not bothered by how he looks, and he sometimes gets angry for no reason.

Attention Deficit Hyperactivity Disorder

ADHD is another disorder that is being diagnosed more commonly these days. A triad of symptoms characterizes ADHD:

- Hyperactivity
- Inattention
- Impulsivity

Generally, it presents in childhood and improves as children age. Very few people will continue to fulfil the criteria in late teens, and the diagnosis of new adult-onset ADHD is rarer. The diagnosis is made following feedback from teachers and parents and is not a condition that can be accurately self-diagnosed through computer software.

Gayatri is a Class 5 student, and her teachers have been complaining to her parents that she is very fidgety (hyperactive) in her class and often speaks out of turn (impulsive). She often makes 'silly' mistakes (inattention) and gets scolded by her teachers and parents.

Obsessive-Compulsive Disorder

OCD is a common mental disorder and has symptoms that include experiencing intrusive, repetitive and irrelevant thoughts. Then these thoughts are usually followed by compulsions to undo the anxiety associated with them.

Arijit tends to wash his hands and belongings repeatedly as he feels dirty (obsessive thought), and unless he washes them at least five times (compulsion), he doesn't think they are clean. He also feels that he has forgotten what he read (obsessive thought) on the previous page, and therefore he has to re-read those pages five times (compulsion) before he can go ahead. These activities are causing him a lot of frustration.

There is a tendency to label people with OCD if they have certain stereotypical behaviours. It is worth remembering that we are all unique people and generally tend to do things differently. If we all did all the same things in a similar manner, then we would all be like robots and lose our uniqueness.

Mental health issues are very prevalent, and mental health should be looked after as much as we look after our physical health. Although we may want others to look after us, our responsibility towards our mental health cannot be negated. Taking care of ourselves and our mental health should be our own priority, above all.

KEY POINTS

How do you maintain healthy mental health?

1. Be mindful of your stressors. There is nobody with no stress; some people are just better at managing them. If you have started to feel tense, then start making a list of your current challenges and try solving them as best as you can, one by one.
2. Add plenty of 'good coping' mechanisms. Every day, try and do something positive for your body. Regular exercise, sport, dance and hobbies go a long way in avoiding feeling stressed and managing stressors better.
3. Try and sleep well. Working more by sleeping less is counterproductive and reduces productivity.
4. Eat healthy. Food can alter our mood. Drinking excess tea or coffee or consuming extra sugar can disrupt sleep and make us feel anxious. Try to eat a healthy and balanced diet. Drink plenty of water and keep yourself hydrated.
5. Avoid alcohol and smoking to manage your mood. Alcohol, smoking and drugs increase the risks of developing mental disorders and worsening mental states. They are considered 'maladaptive coping' mechanisms to manage stress.

6. Add physical exercise or yoga to your routine. There is enough research to suggest that endorphins are released in the brain when we exercise, which makes us feel positive and improves our confidence.
7. Do something you enjoy daily. Try spending some time doing things that make you happy, such as reading a book, listening to your favourite music, watching your favourite show, etc.
8. Get plenty of sunlight. Spending all day inside the house or room generally increases frustration levels. Try to go out for a walk or some activity during the day.
9. Personal connections are essential. Connect with somebody daily, even if it is through a phone. Virtual connections like social media connections, even in the thousands, don't come close to physical connections.
10. Ask for help. We tend to see medical services and seeking medical assistance as reactive rather than proactive. This means that we only respond when things go wrong and don't do enough to prevent diseases from happening. If you feel something is not right, then speak to a doctor sooner. There is enough evidence that a single session with a psychologist or psychiatrist can bring about long-lasting positive changes in a person.

19

SELF-HARM AND SUICIDE

'You have an amazing life, you know it, everyone else knows it, and yet you feel that ending your life makes more sense than living it.'

—SHON MEHTA

Mental health problems are rising in the world, with about one in four people suffering from mental disorders at some point in their lives. According to the WHO, 'Around 20 per cent of the world's children and adolescents have a mental health condition, with suicide the fourth leading cause of death in 15–29-year-olds.'[42]

Haider, a 17-year-old bright student, moved from a small town to a bigger city to prepare for competitive exams. He was the best student at his school, but when he reached his coaching

---

[42]'The World Health Report 2001: Mental Disorders Affect One in Four People', World health Organization, 2001, http://tinyurl.com/222vxajs. Accessed on 3 January 2024.

institute, he felt that everyone else was better than him in studies. He was unable to make friends and felt lonely. His grades started coming down in mock examinations. He was unable to discuss this with his family, as he felt that he would be letting them down. He started self-harming to cope with his distress, and one day he attempted suicide as he felt hopeless. Fortunately, his roommate arrived on time and took him to the hospital, and he physically recovered over the next few days.

His family came to the hospital and took him home. He started seeing a psychologist and psychiatrist, and his mental health steadily improved in a more supportive environment.

Think of some strategies that Haider could have used to manage his situation:	
1	
2	
3	
4	
5	

Haider could have reached out to his teachers in the coaching institute, his parents, or his siblings to share his feelings. He could have asked for help from mental health professionals himself, or his parents or teachers would have helped him seek support for his mental health. It is better to seek help early rather than wait for things to get worse.

Unfortunately, cases like Haider are very common in India, and according to the National Crime Records Bureau (NCRB), over 13,000 students died by suicide in 2022.[43]

The India suicide rate was considered to be around 14.04 per one lakh population in 2019, which is about 49th in the world, but in terms of sheer number of suicides (1,70,924), it was the highest in the world in 2022. These figures do not include suicidal attempts, and they may be up to 20 times more than completed suicides.[44]

Self-Injurious Behaviours (SIB)

Suicidal behaviours and non-accidental self injury (NSSI) are both part of self-injurious behaviours. Suicidal behaviours include suicidal ideas and thoughts, attempted suicides and completed suicides.

NSSI or Deliberate self injury or deliberate self harm (DSH) can be seen as intentional self-injurious behaviour without suicidal intent, like cutting, banging or hitting self, burning or scratching oneself.

---

[43]National Crime Records Bureau, 'Suicides in India', *Accidental Deaths & Suicides in India 2022*, 2022, pp. 196–208, http://tinyurl.com/4z56r6vc. Accessed on 3 January 2024.

[44]Yadav, Suryakant, et al., 'Changing Pattern of Suicide Deaths in India', *The Lancet Regional Health–Southeast Asia*, Vol. 16, 2023, pp. 100265, http://tinyurl.com/kh3rye9. Accessed on 3 January 2024.

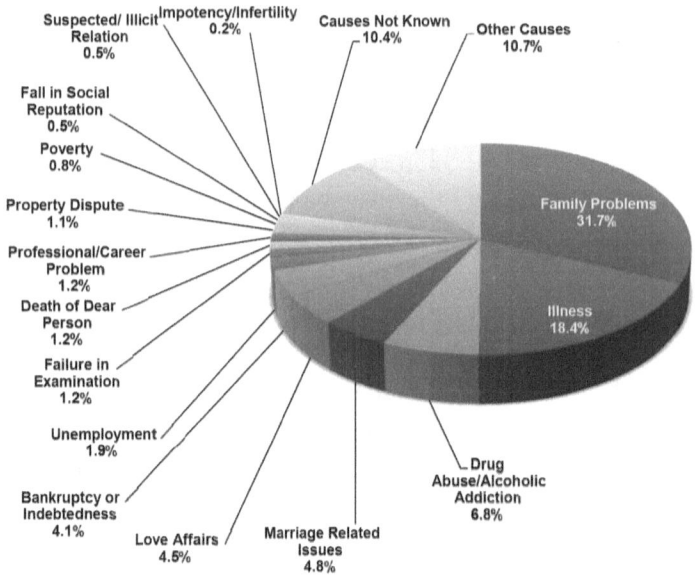

Figure 22: Percentage share of various causes of suicide in India in 2022[45]

As we can see above, the causes of people engaging in suicidal behaviours can be varied, and it is important to look at the causes behind suicidality. People who have attempted suicide before are especially at risk, and the 30–40 per cent who complete suicide have made previous attempts.

---

[45]National Crime Records Bureau, 'Suicides in India', National Crime Records Bureau, 2022, p. 203, http://tinyurl.com/4z56r6vc. Accessed on 3 January 2024.

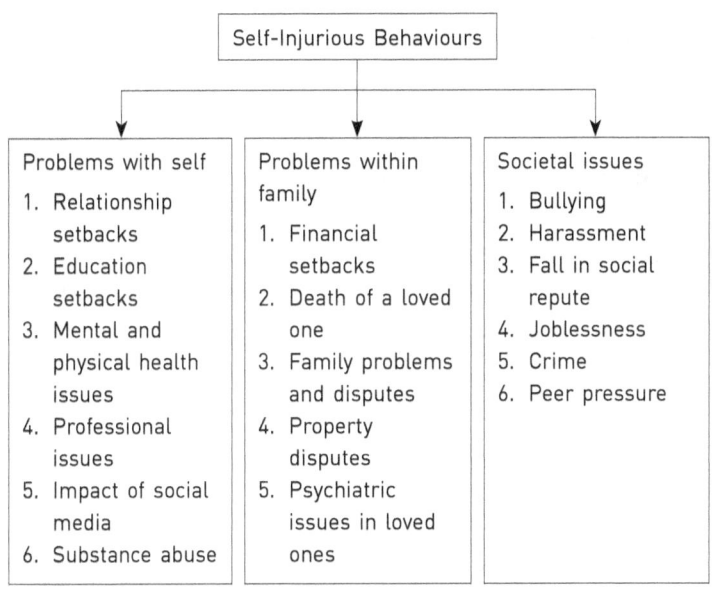

Figure 23: Different aspects of self-injurious behaviours

There can be many reasons for self-injurious behaviour, from rejection and failure to hormonal imbalance. Expressing these thoughts effectively and mindfully is important, but difficult for some people. People may become depressed, and to cope with their emotional turmoil, they may start using escapism in the form of staying away from home, seeking stimulation through excessive socialization, substance abuse, and engaging in risky behaviours. This may increase the risk of self-harm and suicide.

Quite a lot of times, self-harming behaviours are a 'cry for help' when people feel unsupported and hopeless about their life or future.

Possible motives or reasons underlying self-harm:[46]

- To die
- To escape from unbearable anguish
- To change the behaviour of others
- To escape from a situation
- To show desperation to others
- To 'get back at' other people or make them feel guilty
- To gain relief from tension
- To seek help

Reasons for Suicidal Behaviours

1. **Life events and challenges:** Generally, people who self-harm have had difficulties going on for a long time, like a poor home environment, abuse or illnesses but a precipitating event like a relationship breakdown, bereavement or setback in studies may tip them to start self-harming. The focus may be more on the triggering or precipitating factor, but the difficulties may be long-standing.
2. **Maladaptive coping or bad coping skills:** As we discussed in the first chapter of this book, there is no one with no stress, but there are people who manage stress better. Management of stress is based around problem-solving techniques and good coping mechanisms. Deliberate self-harm is considered a bad coping method for dealing with difficulties in life.

---

[46]Hawton, Keith, and Anthony James, 'Suicide and Deliberate Self Harm in Young People', *BMJ*, Vol. 330, No. 7496, 2005, pp. 891–94, http://tinyurl.com/ycxf37y4. Accessed on 3 January 2024.

3. **Bottling-up emotions:** Adolescents and adults who bottle up emotions tend to struggle more. We all have a finite capacity to take on stress or deal with emotions and difficulties. Slowly but surely, this capacity gets overwhelmed, and there is an outburst of anger, grief, anxiety or sadness. The learned helplessness and hopelessness of the situation may cause a person to self-harm.
4. **Impact of social media and mass media**: Social media as discussed previously, helps us connect with like-minded people but can also propagate comparison and jealousy. Social media makes comparison easier and gives it an unsavoury twist, whereby one negates all the positives in their life and strives for what the other person has.

    Everyone wants to feel accepted and would like to stand out from the crowd, which can lead to out-of-character behaviours. Excessive social media use has been linked to increased feelings of loneliness, jealousy, anxiety, depression and reduced social skills.

Bhaskar is an 18-year-old boy in his first year of college. This is the first time he has stayed away from his family in a hostel. He was told by some friends that some anonymous person had written on a social networking site that he was a 'stalker'. There was no way of knowing who did it, and according to him, this was a baseless allegation. All his classmates started shunning him, and he started feeling low in mood while experiencing anxiety episodes and poor sleep. He started self-harming and smoking to manage his emotions.

The portrayal of suicidal behaviour in mass media can influence suicidality in viewers as well. The graphic and detailed descriptions of celebrity suicides can lead to 'copycat' suicides.

> How to spot if someone is struggling:
>
> 1. Withdrawing to one's own room
> 2. Isolating oneself and avoiding people
> 3. Changes in sleep and appetite patterns
> 4. Reduced interaction with family
> 5. Excessive anger
> 6. Excessive use of alcohol, smoke or drugs
> 7. Reduction in academic performance
> 8. Sustained low mood and low motivation

5. **Mental disorders:** Almost any psychiatric illness can increase the risk of self-injurious behaviours; the highest incidence is in depression and alcohol dependence. Poor compliance and continuation of treatment make things worse.
6. **Sociodemographic factors:** Any adversity in life can impact a person's physical and psychological well-being. Financial hardships, natural disasters, migration and poor education levels can cause a predisposition to mental illnesses in the future. A person can experience low self-esteem, hopelessness, helplessness, a feeling of powerlessness or depression. This could potentially lead to them resorting to self-harm as a way to vent out the heavy emotions they are experiencing. A study conducted by Lodebo et al. in 2017 found that 'compared to the highest income category,

adolescents from the lower-income categories were 1.08 to 1.19 times more likely to self-harm.'[47]

7. **Environmental factors and abuse**: Bullying occurs when an individual is subjected to intentional verbal or physical harm that is associated with an unequal power dynamic between the victim and the abuser. Teenagers in complex social environments such as school, sports teams and extracurricular classes might experience unhealthy encounters with bullies. This can appear in the form of verbal abuse, physical abuse or cyberbullying, which refers to bullying over an online platform. However, the form of bullying does not alter its consequences for the victim, as it might lead to suppressed emotions, low self-esteem, low self-confidence, and much more. These difficult feelings about themselves form the basis of mental health struggles with depression and anxiety. One possible explanation for the association between bullying and self-harm is the notion that self-harm serves to cope with intense emotions.

Interventions

Interventions should focus both on the prevention and management of self-injurious behaviours.

---

[47]Lodebo, Bereket T., et al., 'Socioeconomic Position and Self-Harm among Adolescents: A Population-Based Cohort Study in Stockholm, Sweden', *Child and Adolescent Psychiatry and Mental Health*, Vol. 11, No. 46, 2017, http://tinyurl.com/22drdkvy. Accessed on 3 January 2024.

Interventions:

1. **Better mental health awareness:** Help is difficult without awareness and acknowledgment.
2. **Self-help techniques:** Better coping mechanisms, exercise, writing a diary or gratitude journal, speaking to a friend, not bottling-up emotions.
3. **Professional help:** Supportive counselling, family therapy, CBT and DBT techniques.
4. **Medications:** Medicines to manage mood and anxiety.
5. **Inpatient treatment:** In rare cases, inpatient psychiatric treatment may be required.

Prevention

Early detection, improving awareness and improving access to psychological health care become essential parts of the prevention of self-injurious behaviours.

1. **Early detection:** Identification of children at risk; looking at signs of mental struggle like isolation, decreased academic performance, absenteeism, getting into fights at school, etc.
2. **Awareness sessions:** Holding mental health awareness sessions for students, teachers and parents to improve early detection and self-realization of difficulties.
3. **Access to counsellors and therapists:** Offering help and sessions with mental health professionals early can be of much help. This may be in school or in private settings.

Treatment

The treatment is generally tailored to the person and generally includes a combination of the following:

1. **Lifestyle changes:** Lifestyle changes may include taking out time for yourself to engage in relaxation or resilience-increasing activities as discussed and described previously.
2. **Psychotherapy:** It can include simple counselling or more specialized therapeutic techniques like Cognitive Behavioural Therapy (CBT) or Dialectical Behavioural Therapy (DBT). Usually, a series of sessions are required over months.
3. **Medications:** Medications can help and are generally used in combination with lifestyle changes and psychotherapy. Medications can help with anxiety, depression, impulsivity, anger control and sleep. It is important not to self-medicate with medicines or substances but to seek help from qualified doctors in this field.

TIPS FOR PARENTS

1. Do not panic. Your anxiety can worsen your child's anxiety.
2. Be supportive and listen to the child in an unhurried and a sympathetic manner.
3. Try and think of reasons for the self-harm or suicidal behaviours.
4. Encourage the child to express what they are feeling in a non-judgemental manner.
5. Do seek help at the earliest opportunity.
6. There will be ups and downs in recovery and treatment. This may be something that you have to accept and expect.

7. Be consistent with treatment. Even if the child is better, therapy and medications may need to go on for much longer.
8. Remove access to means of self-harm, like limiting access to sharp things and poisons in the house.
9. You many need help too, to manage your emotions.

Self-harm and suicide are extremely concerning entities, and more must be done in the interest of prevention. This can only be done by increasing awareness in schools and easing the accessibility of therapists and counsellors. Furthermore, young people who self-harm must be supported and treated in a non-judgemental way and with empathy.

If you are struggling with suicidal behaviours, or know someone who is, the following helplines may be of use.

1. iCALL: 9152987821/022-25521111
2. Kiran: 18005990019
3. Vandrevala Foundation Crisis Help Line: 9999666555
4. Tele MANAS: 14416/18008914416
5. NIMHANS: 08046110007

KEY POINTS

1. Self-harm and suicidal thoughts are fairly common.
2. Better awareness, early detection and early treatment is paramount for good recovery.
3. The adolescent needs to be supported in an open and non-judgemental manner.
4. Causes for experiencing such strong emotions should be sought.
5. Treatment has to be tailored to the young person's problems and may include several different interventions.

6. A good treatment is multi-disciplinary, i.e., it should include parents, school, psychologist, social workers and psychiatrist, working together with the young person.
7. Other peers in the class or siblings may also need help and support.

AFTERWORD

I want to end this book with the concepts of mental fitness and mental happiness, which this book is based on.

Mental fitness means the ability to take on challenges and ride the tides of life with confidence. Stress is part and parcel of our fast-paced lives; how smoothly we tackle it and also have the required resilience to stressful events constitutes mental fitness.

Another related term is mental happiness. We may have financial happiness; we may have academic or work-related happiness; but mental happiness is something that is not given much importance in our day-to-day hustle. Financial happiness is no good if we are not overall happy in life. Try finding happiness in whatever you do and not just in work or finances.

We all work to live, but we don't live to work. Similarly, people say that they are unhappy with their lives because of unsatisfactory work, and I usually tell them that we all have to work to keep the house running; it is as essential as brushing, feeding and sleeping, but do you get any happiness or joy out of brushing? There are other things in life to seek pleasure and satisfaction from.

Afterword

And what about a person's potential? Generally, your boss tries to motivate you by saying that you have a lot of skills but you are not fulfilling your true potential, and you should work harder and give your work more time. To that, I would say, what about a person's potential as a father, a daughter or a partner? If the worker provides all their time to fulfil their potential at work, they won't achieve their potential in the other roles they play in life. We need to see life as a sum of all parts, not by a biased view of work and work alone.

There is no right or wrong way to live a life, but it is always helpful to take stock once in a while of what you are doing and why you are doing what you do.

I want to finish the book with what my school principal told me when I met him for the first time: 'Work hard, play hard and enjoy yourself.'

My sincere wish is that you have found this book useful and that it will help you make informed decisions in life.

BIBLIOGRAPHY

'Adolescent Sexuality: Talk the Talk Before They Walk the Walk', *healthychildren.org, 2008, http://tinyurl.com/bw4925uw. Accessed on 4 January 2023.*

'Alcohol', *World Health Organization*, 2002, http://tinyurl.com/hzxv2cmr. Accessed on 4 January 2023.

'Cigarettes', *FDA*, http://tinyurl.com/3vsbf2bd. Accessed on 4 January 2024.

Girlhood, Not Motherhood, United Nations Population Fund, 2015, http://tinyurl.com/2c55hne8. Accessed on 3 January 2024.

'Global Health Estimates: Leading Causes of Death', *World Health Organization*, 2020, http://tinyurl.com/msvxccwu. Accessed on 3 January 2023.

'Health Effects of Cigarette Smoking', *CDC*, http://tinyurl.com/4axjkmh6. Accessed on 4 January 2024.

'Hypertension', *World Health Organization*, 2023, http://tinyurl.com/2w3ezzaj. Accessed on 3 January 2024.

'Mental Health of Adolescents', *World Health Organization*, http://tinyurl.com/yeh3rb45. Accessed on 4 January 2024.

'Obesity and Overweight', *World Health Organization*, 2021, http://tinyurl.com/bdbfy5dd. Accessed on 3 January 2024. 'Physical Activity Guidelines for Americans', *health.gov*, 2023, http://tinyurl.

com/hes2t44j. Accessed on 3 January 2024.

'Physical Activity', *World Health Organization*, 2020, http://tinyurl.com/a7c7bu52. Accessed on 3 January 2024.

Suicide Worldwide in 2019: Global Health Estimates, World Health Organization, Geneva, 2021, http://tinyurl.com/56m75hd9. Accessed on 7 Dec 2023

'Suicide', *World Health Organization*, 2023, http://tinyurl.com/yjy3j9ku. Accessed on 4 January 2024.

National Crime Records Bureau, 'Suicides in India', *Accidental Deaths & Suicides in India 2022,* 2022, http://tinyurl.com/4z56r6vc. Accessed on 3 January 2024.

The Global Strategy for Women's, Children's and Adolescents' Health (2016-2030), United Nations Sustainable Development Goals, 2015.

'The Risks of Drinking Too Much', *NHS*, http://tinyurl.com/2etwumtk. Accessed on 4 January 2024.

'The World Health Report 2001: Mental Disorders Affect One in Four People', *World Health Organization*, 28 September 2001, http://tinyurl.com/222vxajs. Accessed on 4 January 2024.

'Tobacco', *World Health Organization*, http://tinyurl.com/z4zna2jh. Accessed on 4 January 2024.

'World Health Organization Definition of Physical Activity', *Public Health*, World Health Organization, 2020,
http://tinyurl.com/5dky4tjm. Accessed on 3 January 2024.

Ajmera, Rachael, 'Glycemic Index: What It Is and How to Use It', *Healthline*, 2020, http://tinyurl.com/3a9d46n3. Accessed on 3 January 2024.

Andover, Margaret S., and Blair W. Morris, 'Expanding and Clarifying the Role of Emotion Regulation in Nonsuicidal Self-Injury', *The Canadian Journal of Psychiatry*, Vol. 59, No. 11, 2014, pp. 569–575, http://tinyurl.com/yvb7d7k7. Accessed on 4 January 2024.

Andreasson S., et al., 'Cannabis and Schizophrenia. A Longitudinal Study of Swedish Conscripts', *The Lancet*, Vol. 330, No. 8574, 1987.

Balhara, Yatan Pal Singh, et al., 'Problematic Internet Use and Its Correlates among Students from Three Medical Schools across Three Countries', *Academic Psychiatry*, Vol. 39, No. 6, 2015, pp. 634–638, http://tinyurl.com/3595bz7v. Accessed 4 January 2024.

Castro, Ángel, et al., 'Childhood Sexual Abuse, Sexual Behavior and Revictimization in Adolescence and Youth: A Mini Review', *Frontiers in Psychology*, Vol. 10, 2019, http://tinyurl.com/4fy2jcvs. Accessed on 4 January 2024.

Chhabria, Anjali, *Death Is Not the Answer: Understanding Suicide and the Ways to Prevent It*, Penguin Books Limited, 2016.

Darroch, Jacqueline E., et al., 'Adding It Up: Costs and Benefits of Meeting the Contraceptive Needs of Adolescents', *Guttmacher Institute*, 2016, http://tinyurl.com/bdyyfea7. Accessed on 3 January 2024.

Diamond, Milton, 'Pornography, Public Acceptance and Sex Related Crime: A Review', *International Journal of Law and Psychiatry*, Vol. 32, No. 5, 2009, pp. 304–314, http://tinyurl.com/mrnhah83. Accessed on 4 January 2024.

Duggan, Maeve, 'Gaming and Gamers', *Pew Research Center:*, 2015, http://tinyurl.com/3pccfdtm. Accessed on 4 January 2024.

Durai, Priya Cinna T, and Dhanya G. Nair, 'Acne Vulgaris and Quality of Life among Young Adults in South India', *Indian Journal of Dermatology*, Vol. 60, No. 1, 2015, pp. 33,

http://tinyurl.com/3bz7d6ca. Accessed on 4 January 2024.

Ewing, John A., 'Detecting Alcoholism', *JAMA*, Vol. 252, No. 14, 1984, pp. 1905, http://tinyurl.com/y4sk6w88. Accessed on 4 January 2024.

Fletcher, James, 'The Worrying Effects of Working More and Sleeping Less', *BBC*, http://tinyurl.com/y2jfw289. Accessed on 3 January 2024.

Ganchimeg, T, et al., 'Pregnancy and Childbirth Outcomes among

Adolescent Mothers: A World Health Organization Multicountry Study', *BJOG: An International Journal of Obstetrics and Gynaecology*, Vol. 121, 2014, pp. 40–8, http://tinyurl.com/2y7mxezr. Accessed on 3 January 2024.

Ghavidel-Heidari, Mahbobe, et al., 'Predictors of Adolescents' Pornography: Level of Sexual Behavior and Family Environment', *Journal of Family and Reproductive Health*, 2012, pp. 165–168, http://tinyurl.com/5n8rbtvk. Accessed on 3 January 2024.

González-Ortega, Eva, and Begoña Orgaz - Baz, 'Minors' Exposure to Online Pornography: Prevalence, Motivations, Contents and Effects', *Anales de Psicología*, Vol. 29, No. 2, 2013,

http://tinyurl.com/mt9yuz62. Accessed on 3 January 2024.

Gorvett, Zaria, 'The Forgotten Medieval Habit of "Two Sleeps"', *BBC*, 10 January 2022, http://tinyurl.com/yc2pvx39. Accessed on 3 January 2024.

Griffiths M.D., 'Technological Addiction', *Clinical Psychology Forum*, Vol. 76, 1995, pp. 14–19.

Hawton, Keith, and Anthony James, 'Suicide and Deliberate Self Harm in Young People', *BMJ*, Vol. 330, No. 7496, 2005, pp. 891–94, http://tinyurl.com/ycxf37y4. Accessed on 3 January 2024.

'Healthy Eating Plate', *The Nutrition Source*, Harvard T.H. Chan School of Public Health, 2011.

Jones, Jeffrey M., 'In U.S., 40% Get Less than Recommended Amount of Sleep', *Gallup*, 19 December 2013, http://tinyurl.com/29hjt3c7. Accessed on 3 January 2024.

Kar, Sujita Kumar, et al., 'Understanding Normal Development of Adolescent Sexuality: A Bumpy Ride', *Journal of Human Reproductive Sciences*, Vol. 8, No. 2, 2015, pp. 70,

http://tinyurl.com/s4r6n322. Accessed on 4 January 2024.

Klonsky, E. David, et al., 'Nonsuicidal Self-Injury: What We Know, and What We Need to Know', *The Canadian Journal of Psychiatry*,

Vol. 59, No. 11, 2014, pp. 565–568, http://tinyurl.com/2hz5uy7u. Accessed on 4 January 2024.

Kundanis, Rose M., 'Children, Teens, Families and Mass Media: The Millennial Generation', *Routledge & CRC Press*, 2003, http://tinyurl.com/436dae4v. Accessed on 3 January 2024.

Laili, Mahsiani Mina, et al., 'Is It Parental Communication, Self-Esteem, or Internet Use That Makes Pornography Behavior in Teenagers? (Cases of Pornography and Porno-Action)', *Journal of Child Development Studies*, Vol. 3, No. 1, 2018, pp. 59–69.

Lee, Hogan H., et al., 'Differences by Sex in Association of Mental Health with Video Gaming or Other Nonacademic Computer Use among US Adolescents', *Preventing Chronic Disease*, Vol. 14, 2017, http://tinyurl.com/2zs2wubw. Accessed on 4 January 2024.

Lim, Megan S.C., et al., 'The Impact of Pornography on Gender-Based Violence, Sexual Health and Well-Being: What Do We Know?', *Journal of Epidemiology and Community Health*, Vol. 70, No. 1, 2015, pp. 3–5, http://tinyurl.com/sp4zxn8x. Accessed on 4 January 2024.

Lodebo, Bereket T., et al., 'Socioeconomic Position and Self-Harm among Adolescents: A Population-Based Cohort Study in Stockholm, Sweden', *Child and Adolescent Psychiatry and Mental Health*, Vol. 11, No. 46, 2017, http://tinyurl.com/22drdkvy. Accessed on 3 January 2024.

Marconi A., et al., 'Meta-Analysis of the Association between the Level of Cannabis Use and Risk of Psychosis', *Schizophrenia Bulletin*, Vol. 42, No. 5, 2016, pp. 1262–69.

Mitchell, D.C., et al., 'Beverage Caffeine Intakes in the U.S.', *Food and Chemical Toxicology*, Vol. 63, 2014, pp. 136–42.

Naci, Huseyin, and John P. A. Ioannidis, 'Comparative Effectiveness of Exercise and Drug Interventions on Mortality Outcomes: Metaepidemiological Study', *British Journal of Sports Medicine*,

Vol. 49, No. 21, 2015, pp. 1414–22, http://tinyurl.com/saehrk7n. Accessed on 3 January 2024.

Neal, Sarah, et al., 'Childbearing in Adolescents Aged 12-15 Years in Low Resource Countries: A Neglected Issue. New Estimates from Demographic and Household Surveys in 42 Countries', *Acta Obstetricia et Gynecologica Scandinavica*, Vol. 91, No. 9, 2012, pp. 1114–18, http://tinyurl.com/3ssre3a4. Accessed on 3 January 2024.

Ohlsson, Claes, et al., 'Secular Trends in Pubertal Growth Acceleration in Swedish Boys Born from 1947 to 1996', *JAMA Pediatrics*, Vol. 173, No. 9, 2019, p. 860, http://tinyurl.com/mr3y3aw8. Accessed on 3 January 2024.

Owens, Eric W., et al., 'The Impact of Internet Pornography on Adolescents: A Review of the Research', *Sexual Addiction & Compulsivity*, Vol. 19, No. 1–2, 2012, pp. 99–122, http://tinyurl.com/5t3npue8. Accessed on 3 January 2024.

Papathanasiou, Ioanna V., and Lahana Eleni, 'Adolescence, Sexuality and Sexual Education', *Health Science Journal*, 2007.

Pirkis, J., et al., 'Media Guidelines on the Reporting of Suicide', *Crisis*, Vol. 27, No. 2, 2006, pp. 82–87.

Price, G.B., 'Alcoholism and Childhood', *British Journal of Inebriety*, Vol. 8, No. 2, 1910, pp. 67–77.

Radhakrishnan, Rajiv, and Chittaranjan Andrade, 'Suicide: An Indian Perspective', *Indian Journal of Psychiatry*, Vol. 54, No. 4, 2012, p. 304, http://tinyurl.com/y7urxwcu. Accessed on 4 January 2024.

Rastogi, Vipul, 'Time to Rethink Maslow's Hierarchy of Needs', *The Times of India*, 2015, http://tinyurl.com/y9khry53. Accessed on 3 January 2024.

Reimers, C.D., et al., 'Does Physical Activity Increase Life Expectancy? A Review of the Literature', *Journal of Aging Research*, 2012, http://tinyurl.com/y83ekn2v. Accessed on 3 January 2024.

Ross, Shana, and Nancy Heath, 'A Study of the Frequency of Self-Mutilation in a Community Sample of Adolescents', *Journal of Youth and Adolescence*, Vol. 31, No. 1, 2002, pp. 67–77, http://tinyurl.com/3dz39yaw. Accessed on 4 January 2024.

Roth, T., 'Insomnia: Definition, Prevalence, Etiology and Consequences', *Journal of Clinical Sleep Medicine*, Vol. 3, 2007.

Shaw, Mary, Richard Mitchell and Danny Dorling, 'Time for a Smoke? One Cigarette Reduces Your Life by 11 Minutes', *BMJ*, Vol. 320, No. 7226, 2000, p. 53.

Siomos, Konstantinos, et al., 'Evolution of Internet Addiction in Greek Adolescent Students over a Two Year Period the Impact of Parental Bonding', *European Child & Adolescent Psychiatry*, Vol. 21, No. 4, 2012, pp. 211–219, http://tinyurl.com/bzz3aw7k. Accessed on 4 January 2024.

Sridharan, Rajiv, and Rani Maria George, 'Factors Aggravating or Precipitating Acne in Indian Adults: A Hospital-Based Study of 110 Cases', *Indian Journal of Dermatology*, Vol. 63, No. 4, 2018, pp. 328, http://tinyurl.com/3ruzdbjf. Accessed on 3 January 2024.

Tulloch, Trisha, and Miriam Kaufman, 'Adolescent Sexuality', *Pediatrics in Review*, 2023, http://tinyurl.com/58yb7b6x. Accessed on 3 January 2024.

Vaishnav, Mrugesh, et al., *IPS Textbook of Sexuality and Sexual Medicine* Jaypee Brothers Medical Publishers, 2022, pp. 567–72.

Whitlock J., et al., 'Self-Injurious Behaviours in College Population', *Pediatrics*, Vol. 117, 2006.

Yadav, Suryakant, et al., 'Changing Pattern of Suicide Deaths in India', *The Lancet Regional Health–Southeast Asia*, Vol. 16, 2023. http://tinyurl.com/kh3rye9. Accessed on 3 January 2024.

Young, Kimberly, 'Internet Addiction a New Clinical Phenomenon and Its Consequences', *American Behavioral Scientist*, Vol. 48, No. 4, 2004, http://tinyurl.com/pnppsta4. Accessed on 4 January 2024.

ACKNOWLEDGEMENTS

I have tried to write all about what I would have loved to know when I was growing up. The example in Chapter 3 of the 24-year-old who didn't know what debit and credit were, was me. I wrote the book keeping not only the young adults in mind but grown-ups as well who may also find many things of interest in this book.

This book has taken me a better part of two years to conceptualize and write, and includes my experience of the last twenty years spent working in this field. This book is inspired by all the young people I meet every day, and that experience has guided me to pick up the topics covered in this book.

Firstly, I want to thank my colleagues who have taken out time to contribute their time and efforts to this book; without their contribution, this work would have felt incomplete. I would also take this opportunity to apologize to them for pushing them to write as soon as they could.

I would then like to thank my colleagues in the Division of Mental Health, Medanta, who were constant supporters and read the manuscript several times, and advised changes. A shout-out to Dr Saurabh Mehrotra, Dr Priyanka Gupta, Ms Akanksha Batra, Dr Natasha Kumar and Ms Ishita Bhatt.

My special thanks to the young people who helped shape the book and made it what it is today. A special mention goes to Anoushka Jain, Khushi Rastogi, Himani Agarwal, Ananya Garg—who were brimming with ideas—for going through this manuscript many times. They helped make the book more user-friendly and were very honest in their appraisal of the book.

A further thanks to Ms Shilpa Rastogi, Mr Shobhit Agarwal and Mrs Nidhi Rastogi for giving a teacher's and a parent's perspective on the book. It was really helpful.

A big thanks to my publisher, Rupa Publications, and especially to Mr Kapish Mehra, for his ideas on making the content more engaging for the readers.

A super thanks to friends around me who were all very encouraging and helped me in different ways; a special mention to Ritesh, Amit, Avantika, Rachita, Anuj, Reetika, Saket, Roopali, Nitin, Geetika, Aditya, Divya, Atul, Kritika, Mudit, Nitin, Tarang and Jatin. You may have found some of their names in vignettes in the book.

A very special thanks to some fellow professionals who have helped write certain sections of the book. Their assistance has made this book feel complete, as there are certain sections that do not usually fall under my areas of expertise.

Dr Shradha Chaudhary, senior consultant in the obstetrics and gynaecology department, Medanta Hospital, Gurgaon, for helping with the chapter on women's health and contraception.

Dr Feroz Amir Zafar, senior consultant in the uroandrology department for help with the chapter on sex, sexuality and sexual orientation.

Ms Ritu S Dhingra, consulting psychologist, career planner, international universities' guidance and counselling expert for all her help with the chapter on career choices and how to make them.

Dr Anjali Chhabaria, senior consultant psychiatrist and psychotherapist, Mind Temple, Mumbai, for help with the chapter on suicide and self-harm.

Dr Saurabh Mehrotra, associate director in the mental health department, Medanta, for helping with the chapter on Internet and screen addiction.

Bhavya Malhotra, MSc in food and nutrition, PhD fellow in population health informatics. Her help with the chapter on nutrition for adolescents was invaluable.

Vineet Nanda runs SIFT Capital, a wealth management business, and his input on the chapter 'The Question of Money' was extremely valuable.

Dr Seemant Singh, MD, family physician with fellowship in sports medicine has contributed greatly to the chapter 'Physical Health, Exercise and Supplements'.

Finally, a big thank you to my wife, Niharika and son, Parth, for bearing with me while I wrote this book. This book really ate into our personal family time.

www.ingramcontent.com/pod-product-compliance
Lightning Source LLC
Chambersburg PA
CBHW020329170426
43200CB00006B/321